SpringerBriefs in Applied Sciences an

PoliMI SpringerBriefs

Series Editors

Barbara Pernici, Politecnico di Milano, Milano, Italy

Stefano Della Torre, Politecnico di Milano, Milano, Italy

Bianca M. Colosimo, Politecnico di Milano, Milano, Italy

Tiziano Faravelli, Politecnico di Milano, Milano, Italy

Roberto Paolucci, Politecnico di Milano, Milano, Italy

Silvia Piardi, Politecnico di Milano, Milano, Italy

Springer, in cooperation with Politecnico di Milano, publishes the PoliMI Springer-Briefs, concise summaries of cutting-edge research and practical applications across a wide spectrum of fields. Featuring compact volumes of 50 to 125 (150 as a maximum) pages, the series covers a range of contents from professional to academic in the following research areas carried out at Politecnico:

- Aerospace Engineering
- Bioengineering
- Electrical Engineering
- Energy and Nuclear Science and Technology
- Environmental and Infrastructure Engineering
- Industrial Chemistry and Chemical Engineering
- Information Technology
- Management, Economics and Industrial Engineering
- Materials Engineering
- Mathematical Models and Methods in Engineering
- Mechanical Engineering
- Structural Seismic and Geotechnical Engineering
- Built Environment and Construction Engineering
- Physics
- Design and Technologies
- Urban Planning, Design, and Policy

http://www.polimi.it

Monica Bordegoni · Marina Carulli · Elena Spadoni

Prototyping User eXperience in eXtended Reality

POLITECNICO
MILANO 1863

Monica Bordegoni
Department of Mechanical Engineering
Politecnico di Milano
Milan, Italy

Marina Carulli
Department of Mechanical Engineering
Politecnico di Milano
Milan, Italy

Elena Spadoni
Department of Design
Politecnico di Milano
Milan, Italy

ISSN 2191-530X   ISSN 2191-5318 (electronic)
SpringerBriefs in Applied Sciences and Technology
ISSN 2282-2577   ISSN 2282-2585 (electronic)
PoliMI SpringerBriefs
ISBN 978-3-031-39682-3   ISBN 978-3-031-39683-0 (eBook)
https://doi.org/10.1007/978-3-031-39683-0

This Springer imprint is published by the registered company Springer Nature Switzerland AG
The registered company address is: Gewerbestrasse 11, 6330 Cham, Switzerland

Contents

Chapter 1
Introduction

Abstract This chapter provides insights into the dynamic nature of product design and the key factors influencing consumer perceptions and preferences in the modern era. It explores the multidimensional field of product design, which combines engineering, design, psychology, and other disciplines to create new products. It emphasizes the importance of understanding the concept of a product, which comprises both tangible and intangible elements that provide value to consumers. Today's products are complex systems that constantly evolve due to advancing technology and the demands of customers. The chapter discusses the shift in customer preferences towards personalized products and the challenges faced in manufacturing customized items, and highlights the three primary attributes of products: functions, style, and usability. The chapter also emphasizes the increasing importance of customization and personalization in product design, and explores the significance of efficient product development processes to meet market demands and user expectations.

Product design is a fascinating field with many dimensions that combines elements of engineering, design, psychology, and other fields and that can bring together individuals from diverse backgrounds and cultures to create new products, whether they are variations of existing ones or entirely original. To fully comprehend the role of product design in modern industry, it is essential to have a full understanding of what a product is.

A product can be considered as a combination of tangible and intangible elements that are sold for a monetary exchange, but that can also provide value to consumers. Today's products are intricate systems that are continuously evolving due to advancing technology on one side and more demanding customers on the other. For example, as technology advances, smartphone manufacturers are continually adding new features and capabilities to their devices to meet the demands of consumers; with the rise of electric and self-driving cars, the automotive industry is undergoing a rapid transformation, where car manufacturers are constantly updating their systems to keep pace with the latest technological advances and meet the demands of increasingly tech-savvy customers.

© The Author(s), under exclusive license to Springer Nature Switzerland AG 2023
M. Bordegoni et al., *Prototyping User eXperience in eXtended Reality*,
PoliMI SpringerBriefs, https://doi.org/10.1007/978-3-031-39683-0_1

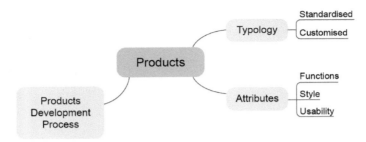

Fig. 1.1 Products' typology and attributes

To expand our understanding of products, let us begin by examining their typology and attributes (Fig. 1.1).

Customers' preferences have shifted in recent years. Previously, products were widely available, mass-produced items. Today, there is a growing desire for personalized products, including shoes, t-shirts, bags, jewelry, furniture, cars, and more that can be customized in-store or online. As a result, many companies have adapted to design and produce small quantities of products tailored to individual customers' needs. However, manufacturing customized products bring issues and challenges. First, customizing products for individual customers can be more expensive compared to mass-producing standard products, as it requires more time, resources, and specialized equipment. The process of producing small quantities of customized products can take longer, as it requires a more complex production process and requires more time for design, prototyping and testing. Furthermore, designing and producing small quantities of customized products can be difficult to scale up as the demand increases, as it requires a significant increase in resources and specialized equipment. Finally, companies that specialize in producing small quantities of customized products may face competition from mass producers, who are able to offer lower prices and a wider range of products. Despite these challenges, many companies continue to focus on producing small quantities of customized products, as they believe that it is a key to delivering a unique and high-quality customer experience.

Regarding attributes, the three primary attributes of products are functions, style, and usability, which are hereafter detailed.

Functions refer to the technical operations performed by the product. Fully understanding how products function is crucial in the development of new products [1]. For example, a squeezer can be evaluated based on its ability to extract citrus juices. Technology is closely related to the development and function of products, as it plays a significant role in determining the capabilities and performance of the product. With the advancement of technology, new products can be developed with better and more complex functions, and existing products can be improved to be more efficient and user-friendly. Technology also enables the creation of new materials that can be used in product development. Thus, a deep understanding of technology is essential for developing innovative and high-quality products. However, it is important to note that having advanced technology at the core of a product does not guarantee commercial success. In fact, the intense competition in the market makes it challenging for a company to gain an advantage solely through technology.

Style refers to the visual appearance or outer appearance of a product and provides aesthetic value to consumers. In product design, styles often embody specific principles and techniques for achieving design objectives. Fashion clothing and accessories are a prime example of the importance of style in product design. Different fashion styles, such as minimalism or maximalism, embody specific design principles and techniques to create unique and aesthetically pleasing products. Consumers choose clothing and accessories based on the style that aligns with their personal taste and aesthetic preferences.

The third property is *usability*. According to ISO, usability is defined as "The extent to which a product can be used by specified users to achieve specified goals with effectiveness, efficiency, and satisfaction in a specified context of use." [2]. Usability includes aspects such as ease of use, interactivity, learnability, and content relevance. For example, in a mobile app for online shopping usability refers to the extent to which customers can effectively search and purchase products, efficiently navigate the app, and be satisfied with the shopping experience within the context of using a smartphone. Usability is closely related to User eXperience (UX), which encompasses the emotions and attitudes a user has while interacting with a product, system, or service [3]. An example of user experience for a consumer product is a person using a smart home speaker. If the speaker is easy to set up, intuitive to use and responds accurately to voice commands, the user is likely to have a positive experience and emotions towards the device. On the other hand, if the speaker is difficult to set up, has poor voice recognition and frequently fails to respond to commands, the user may have a negative experience and emotions towards the device. In this case, the usability of the smart home speaker directly impacts the user's overall user experience.

Nowadays, people do not just value a product based on its function, but also consider style and usability. In fact, people often place a greater emphasis on the product's pleasantness and ease of use and assume that it will function properly. The ability to customize both the appearance and functionality of a product is highly valued by users. For example, phone manufacturers often advertise the ability to change phone cases and wallpapers as a way to personalize the look of the device. This customization is highly valued by users as it allows them to make the phone their own. Some car manufacturers offer options to customize the appearance of a vehicle, such as different color options or custom decals. This allows the user to make the car reflect their personal style, which is a highly valued feature for many buyers. Furniture retailers often offer the ability to customize the look of a piece of furniture by selecting different fabrics, colors, and finishes. This customization is seen as a valuable feature by users because it allows them to create a piece that fits their personal style and taste.

Given the context of modern product expectations, the process for product development must be highly efficient to quickly bring competitive products to market. Additionally, these products must perform well and meet the needs and preferences of users. The steps involved in product development are addressed in the next section.

1.1 Product Development—When Testing Matters

The product development process involves turning a market opportunity into a commercially available product. It encompasses various activities that a company uses to create, design, and bring a product to market. The company must approach the process from both the customer's point of view and the idea's creation, which can lead to a repetitive process to find the optimal balance between the two perspectives. The process for product development is characterized by several phases, a development team and related disciplines, as shown in Fig. 1.2.

Historically, product design was centered on technical features and companies marketed the product solely based on its technology. Style and usability were given secondary consideration, viewed as mere embellishments rather than critical components of a product's success. Only in recent years has design gained equal importance in product development, reflecting the shift in customer evaluation of products, which now encompasses ergonomics and style as well as technology.

Due to the increasing complexity of products, product development *teams* now consist of two roles: engineers who handle technical aspects and industrial designers who primarily focus on style and usability.

Engineers, including mechanical, electrical, materials, software, and manufacturing engineers, provide an instrumental contribution in developing the technologies and manufacturing processes that allow the product to achieve its form, performance, weight, etc.

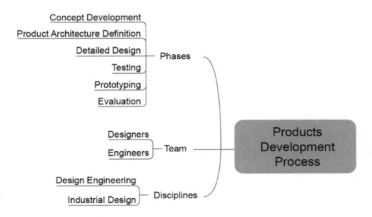

Fig. 1.2 Overview of the product development process

Fig. 1.3 Challenges related to the development of products

Industrial Designers are more focused on the definition of the size and shape of products, and human factors. Industrial designers are primarily responsible for the aspects of a product that relate to the user's experience—the product's aesthetic appeal (how it looks, sounds, feels, and smells) and its functional interfaces (how it is used).

The two roles of engineers and industrial designers correspond to two disciplines: Design Engineering and Industrial Design. *Design Engineering* (DE) converts the design of a product from a concept or prototype into a functional, customer-appealing item. It is a process used by engineers to create functional products and processes [4].

Industrial Design (ID), on the other hand, is a professional service that focuses on enhancing the product's aesthetic appeal and functionality. ID involves creating and developing concepts and specifications that improve the function, value, and appearance of products and systems, benefiting both the user and the manufacturer [4].

The development of products is accompanied by several *challenges*, which are listed in Fig. 1.3.

The complexity of products has been a growing trend for the past decade and remains a major challenge for companies. This *complexity* arises from several factors, such as the large number of parts and components in product architecture, which has impact on the designs, particularly on the mechanical design, and the growing integration of electronics and software in response to market demands for more connected and smart products. Additionally, the use of new materials for improved aesthetics and performance also adds to the complexity. To effectively manage the development of these complex products, companies must have the appropriate methods and tools in place.

Differentiating a brand from its competition is becoming more challenging. Differentiation refers to creating a unique and recognizable element that makes a brand more appealing to consumers than others. With technology no longer being the sole or primary differentiation factor, companies need to focus on unique elements that make their products worth buying, such as innovation, high quality, reliability, rich functionality and features, style, usability, and connected services. These elements play a crucial role in competitive differentiation.

Despite customers demanding *lower costs*, they also want products with *increased functionality, features, and aesthetics.* Consumers expect products to be attractive, user-friendly, and smart. Smart products, which offer multiple features in one device, are rapidly growing in popularity and differentiate from traditional products. An example of a smart product that meets consumers' expectations for being attractive, user-friendly, and smart is a smartwatch. A smartwatch combines multiple features such as fitness tracking, messaging, voice-activated virtual assistants, and mobile payments into one device. It is designed to be worn on the wrist and is highly customizable with different watch faces and bands, making it attractive to a wide range of consumers. Additionally, the user interface is designed to be intuitive and easy to use, allowing users to access its features with just a few taps or swipes.

Smart products are personalized, adaptive, proactive, and situated, combining a physical object with additional services, such as smart light bulbs, bathroom scales, and watches. Despite their added value in terms of functionality, aesthetics, and services, customers are not willing to pay high prices unless they are from established brands. Thus, companies must design unique and innovative products that follow the trend of smart products while keeping costs low.

Another challenge facing companies is limited resources, particularly *limited time* for product development. Companies face pressure to get new products to market quickly, resulting in shortened development schedules and a need for a faster time-to-market. This leaves limited time for the development teams to complete their tasks, requiring an optimized process and well-coordinated development phases. Quick decisions must also be made, ensuring things are done right the first time.

The *lack of tolerance for design flaws* is an additional challenge. The tolerance for design flaws is low due to customer expectations for high-quality products. The design process can sometimes lead to flaws if designers do not meet the customer's standards or have a different perception of quality [5]. Many (if not most) products which we are familiar with today have a long history of previously flawed designs [6]. Testing and evaluation during product development play a crucial role in creating appealing and functional products that meet customer expectations, as will be discussed in the following sections.

The final challenge in product design that we consider is *sustainability.* Sustainability encompasses ecological, social, and economic aspects and requires a holistic approach to achieve lasting prosperity. Although relatively new in the product design field, designing for sustainability involves creating products and services that enable users to carry out their daily activities in a way that reduces negative impact on the environment, economy, and society. Design for sustainable behavior is a user-centered approach that aims to create conditions for a sustainable lifestyle. Selvefors and Renström state that "Design for sustainable behaviour is a user- and use-centered design approach that can be applied to design products and services that create preconditions for a sustainable everyday life." and also "The approach empowers design practitioners to address the impacts of their designs during the use stage of products' lifecycles." [7]. To effectively design for sustainable behavior, it is crucial to have a deep understanding of users, their habits, and interaction behaviors and the contextual factors that influence their ability to act sustainably. This requires

Table 1.1 Challenges and proposed solutions

#	Challenges	Proposed solutions
1	Product complexity	Proper design methods, right design tools
2	Competitive differentiation	Design: style, usability, services
3	Richer product functionality	Design of smart products
4	Lower cost products	Lower development costs
5	Limited time to develop innovative products	Well-coordinated phases Quick decisions taken Things are right and done right
6	Lack of tolerance for design faults	Test and evaluation of designs
7	Sustainability	Proper users' studies and tests

comprehensive user studies that go beyond just understanding what people do and think, but also what they know, feel, and dream about.

Table 1.1 provides a summary of the previously mentioned challenges and possible solutions. The solutions often involve design and *evaluation methods and tools*, which are the focus of this book as they play a crucial role in product development.

At a high-level overview, the product development process can be divided into four main stages: concept development, product architecture definition, detailed design, and testing (Fig. 1.2). The focus of this book is mainly on concept development and testing.

1.2 Concept Design—The Place for Testing

In this book, our focus is on concept design, which centers around the work of industrial designers and common design methods. Specifically, we are interested in exploring the design of those products that have interaction as a key aspect.

A *concept* refers to a detailed explanation of a product's form, function, and features, which is usually developed through market research and analysis of rival products. This is accompanied by a set of specifications. Typically, the concept design phase takes place at the beginning of product development, where the needs of the target market are determined, several product concepts are created and evaluated, and one or more concepts are chosen for further advancement and examination (Fig. 1.4).

The process of creating new products involves overcoming problems and challenges, which may be poorly defined or even unknown. One of the key approaches used to address problem-solving in design is the Design Thinking model, which was introduced by the Hasso-Plattner Institute of Design at Stanford (d.school) [8]. The Design Thinking methodology, which will be extensively described in Chap. 2, is based on five stages, including: *Empathise, Define, Ideate, Prototype* and *Test*. Hereafter the five stages are shortly described, to introduce the concepts and models that will be discussed in more details in the following chapters.

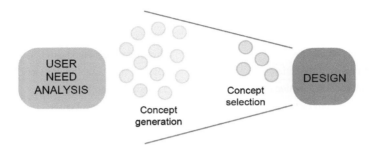

Fig. 1.4 Concept design as a converging process

Once the data has been collected, the design team uses it to perform a thorough analysis and define the key problems (*Define* stage), which are then expressed as a problem statement. The information gathered during the user needs analysis is organized into a list of requirements, specifying what the product must do. These requirements can be prioritized based on their importance. With this information, the design team can begin developing product concepts.

After a thorough comprehension and analysis of user needs and a well-defined problem statement, the design team proceeds to the *Concept* Design stage. Here, the focus is on generating ideas and finding new solutions to the problem. Concept Design involves outlining the general idea of a product that addresses the requirements, and specific user needs in the market. The objective of concept generation is to explore potential solutions, including external research and creative problem-solving techniques. In this stage of product development, various aspects, such as user experience, usability, styling, and technology are considered. It is crucial to generate as many ideas and potential solutions as possible to cover all possibilities and leave nothing unexplored. This often results in a set of concepts, which are usually presented by designers through texts, sketches, or 3D models. Afterwards, the product concepts are evaluated to eliminate the less promising ones. Eventually, one or a few concepts will be chosen for refinement and further development. The approach for selecting the final concept involves evaluating how well it meets the needs, characteristics, and requirements of the users.

The next step in product development is *prototyping*, where the ideas and solutions generated in the concept design stage are put to the test. Prototyping involves creating models of the product concepts to evaluate their effectiveness in meeting users' needs, determining their market potential, and identifying any shortcomings that require improvement. These prototypes are often low-cost, scaled-down, and simplified versions of the final product, with some or all of its features, and are shown to the design team or outside stakeholders for further evaluation and selection of the best solution [4, 9].

For interactive products like consumer goods, evaluating feedback from potential users and the user experience is crucial [10]. Through prototyping, in the *Test* phase, designers can test users' reactions early in the design process. If the response is negative, previous steps may need to be repeated or, in extreme cases, the product development may be discontinued. Testing how real users interact with and feel about the product is essential to avoid market failures and ultimately saves time and money by identifying issues sooner rather than later.

The *Design Thinking approach*, like other concept design methodologies, is an ongoing process that requires continual refinement [11]. It is rare for the process to move in a linear, step-by-step manner, as results from the testing stage are used to improve the understanding of users, their behavior, and the product's conditions of use. The process is often non-linear, and activities may overlap, requiring iterations. New information or results may arise at any point that might necessitate revisiting earlier steps before moving forward.

The use of concept design methods is growing in popularity as companies increasingly rely on design to both meet customer needs and set their products apart from competitors. The user experience has become a key factor in adding value to products, making it a central focus in the design process for many products. To ensure that the design concepts accurately meet user needs and functional requirements, prototyping and testing are crucial steps in the design of new products.

The book is structured into two main sections. The first section (Chaps. 2–4) provides foundational knowledge on three essential topics closely related to the design of interactive products. Chapter 2 delves into the significance of user experience in interactive products and explores various methods for designing user experiences. Chapter 3 focuses on prototyping, offering an overview of different prototyping methods and tools. In Chap. 4, the emphasis shifts to technological aspects, specifically the utilization of eXtended Reality (XR) technologies, which play a significant role in creating virtual prototypes.

The second section of the book (Chaps. 5–8) presents a series of case studies that demonstrate the application of prototyping methods and XR technologies to test novel ideas and solutions during the early conceptual phase of product design. Chapter 5 introduces the methodology employed for implementing the showcased use cases. Chapters 6–8 showcase case studies involving Augmented Reality technology, addressing areas such as sustainability promotion, multisensory applications utilizing extended reality, and applications that bridge the gap between reality and virtuality using Augmented Reality, Virtual Reality, and eXtended Reality technologies. In the concluding chapter (Chap. 9), the book provides a summary of the key findings and valuable insights obtained from the utilization of eXtended Reality to enhance user experience. Additionally, the chapter explores the outcomes of testing various applications using the prototyping methodology. By examining these findings, the book offers a comprehensive understanding of the benefits and challenges associated with integrating XR technologies into the design and testing processes, ultimately contributing to the advancement of interactive product development.

References

1. Aurisicchio M, Eng NL, Ortíz Nicolás JC, Childs PRN, Bracewell RH (2011) On the functions of products. In: Proceedings of the 18th international conference on engineering design, vol 10
2. ISO 9241. https://www.iso.com. Last accessed 15 May 2023
3. Norman D (2017) The design of everyday things: revised and expanded edition. MIT Press
4. Ulrich K, Eppinger S, Yang MC (2019) Product design and development, 7th edn. Mc Graw Hill
5. Gries B, Blessing L (2006) Design flaws: flaws by design? In: Proceedings of international design conference—DESIGN 2006
6. Petroski H (1992) The evolution of useful things. Vintage Books, New York
7. Selvefors A, Renström S (2018) Design for sustainable behaviour, 2018. https://sustainabilityg uide.eu/methods/design-sustainable-behaviour/. Last access 15 May 2023
8. Hasso-Plattner Institute of Design Homepage. https://engineering.stanford.edu/get-involved/ give/hasso-plattner-institute-design. Last access 15 May 2023
9. Bordegoni M, Rizzi C (eds) Innovation in product design—from CAD to virtual prototyping. Springer-Verlag, London
10. Goodman E, Kuniavsky M, Moed A (2012) Observing the user experience: a practitioner's guide to user research, 2nd edn. Elsevier, Amsterdam
11. den Dekker T (2020) Design thinking, 1st edn. Taylor and Francis, London

Chapter 2
User Experience and User Experience Design

Abstract This chapter provides an overview of the fundamental concepts, methodologies, and interdisciplinary nature of User eXperience Design (UX Design). UX Design is a multidisciplinary field that focuses on creating meaningful and valuable experiences for users. This chapter explores the concept of experience and its relation to perception, emotions, and individual needs. It discusses the User Centered Design (UCD) philosophy, which places the user at the center of the design process. The chapter outlines the four main phases of the UCD process: specifying the user and context of use, specifying user requirements, producing design solutions, and evaluating designs. It emphasizes the importance of user participation throughout the design process and highlights various qualitative and quantitative methods used in each phase. The chapter also introduces different models and frameworks, including the Double Diamond model and the Design Thinking model, which provide structured approaches to problem-solving and innovation. Additionally, it addresses the misconception that UX Design is limited to digital products and emphasizes the broader scope of the field, encompassing both digital and physical interactions.

The discourse about User Experience Design, typically referred to as UX Design, starts with a general definition of experience, which can be formulated as the way people perceive things. A more accurate definition of experience was formulated by the International Standard Organization as "a person's perceptions and responses that result from the use or anticipated use of a product, system or service" [1].

Perception is closely related to the process of acquiring knowledge of something by doing, seeing, or feeling. Therefore, this definition highlights the impact of an experience on the user's emotional and individual sphere. Individuals have subjective and personal experiences concerning the world and events that occur in their life. Experiences involve all senses, feelings, evaluation, memory and depend on many aspects, such as individual physical characteristics, culture, social interaction, environment, and context. The user's experience can be related to the person's needs and motivations. Consequently, an experience is considered valuable only if it is perceived as meaningful.

Another definition of experience is given by P. Newbery and K. Farnham as "the set of information you have noticed and stored, along with your emotional and rational

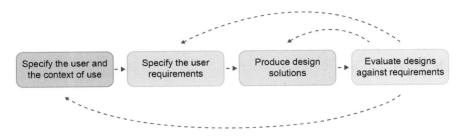

Fig. 2.1 The four phases of the UCD practice [1]

responses that arose from the process of receiving the information and making sense of it at the moment of occurrence." [2]. This definition well correlates an experience and personal elements like emotions, perceptions, physical and psychological responses, behaviours, and needs.

Referring to the industrial design field, the Nielsen Norman Group defines the experience as including all the aspects of the interaction between the user and the company, its services, and its products [3].

On the basis of these assumptions, the UX Design focuses on every element, task, and feeling that the user perceives to deliver the most meaningful experience with the goal of creating efficient, pleasant and relevant products. Good UX Design must create positive experiences for the users by anticipating and fulfilling their needs, through each step of the interaction. In the initial phase of product ideation, sometimes the users' needs are known, in other cases they are unknown or not fully explicit, meaning that the users may not be conscious about them. Thus, the role of the designer is to foresee and anticipate the needs of the users, by taking their point of view.

The UX Design focuses primarily on the users, their behaviours and feelings for delivering the best experiences for them when using and interacting with the designed products and digital applications. This practice derives from the User Centered Design (UCD) philosophy introduced by Norman [4]. UCD is a design process in which designers focus on the users and their needs in each phase of the process. Said from another perspective, the user is always at the center of the design activities. In the UCD practice, the design teams involve users throughout the design process using a variety of research and design methods, to create highly usable and accessible products specifically created for their needs [5]. Therefore, cultivating empathy with the user is a fundamental aspect of UCD.

According to ISO 9241-210 [1], the UCD process is organized into four main phases: *Specify the user and the context of use, Specify the user requirements, Produce design solutions, and Evaluate designs against requirements,* as shown in Fig. 2.1.

- *Specify the user and the context of use*: This first phase focuses on identifying the individuals who will utilize the product and gaining an understanding of their needs, behaviors, motivations, and challenges.

- *Specify the user requirements*: This phase entails comprehending the user's expectations in relation to the project goals and establishing appropriate metrics to measure progress.
- *Produce design solutions*: By considering the aforementioned guidelines, this step aims to determine the product's features and assets.
- *Evaluate designs against requirements*: This analysis involves examining preliminary design options to determine if they effectively meet the user requirements.

The design process is typically iterative, where the convergence toward the ideal solution is reached after a refinement of the initial idea, based on subsequent evaluations. Similarly, UCD is an iterative process, where the phases can be repeated leading up to and post-delivery. For example, after the evaluation phase the design may require a revision; the implementation of the design idea is often subjected to several evaluations.

The users participate to many stages of the UCD process. The participation of the users in these activities is managed and organised meticulously by using different methods and tools.

In the first two phases, the data related to user's needs and expectations are collected mainly through *qualitative* methods, used to develop a deep understanding of the user. The methods typically used are brainstorming, interviews, questionnaires, focus groups, on-site observations, while useful tools are represented by user personas and UX maps, such as the user journey map. When beneficial, extreme users, who are people on either end of the spectrum of users of a product or application, are involved in examining unusual behaviors and attitudes.

In the third phase, related to the design solutions many *qualitative* and *quantitative* methods are adopted, starting from the defined requirements. These methods mainly consist in producing user interaction flow, system architecture, design system definition, wireframing and prototyping.

In the last phase, users take part in the evaluation of the various design alternatives that are proposed by the design team through different testing methods, organized by using prototypes or simulations.

Even if the users' research is an important part in UX Design and in UCD, the design team must also deal with many other factors, for planning and framing the whole system. In fact, UX Design can be considered as an "umbrella" process, covering a wide range of aspects, involving stakeholders, researchers, designers, developers and other members across different areas of the design process.

In this view, Mesut [6] proposes to organize UX Design into four main disciplines, using a Quadrant Model (Fig. 2.2): Experience Strategy (ExS), Interaction Design (IxD), User Research (UR) and Information Architecture (IA).

- *Experience Strategy* is a holistic business strategy, incorporating both the customers' needs and those of the company.
- *Interaction Design* looks at how the user interacts with a product and its specific elements.

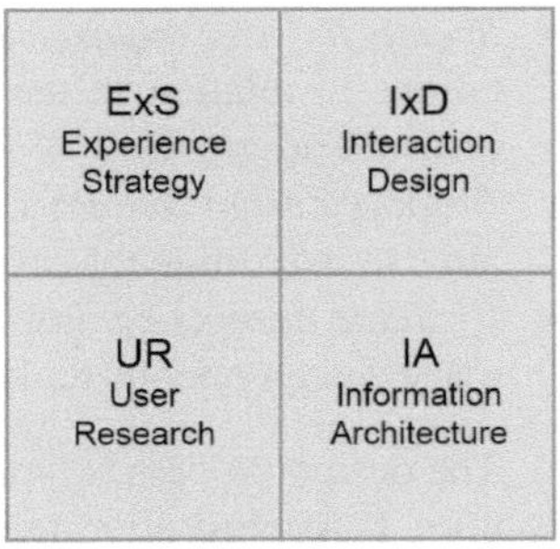

Fig. 2.2 UX design
disciplines: the quadrant
model [6]

ExS Experience Strategy	IxD Interaction Design
UR User Research	IA Information Architecture

- *User Research* aims to gather both qualitative and quantitative data about the user
  and use those to make good design decisions.
- *Information Architecture* is the practice of organizing the gathered information
  and content in a meaningful and accessible way.

Each of these four disciplines can be further organized into sub-disciplines. In fact,
the UX design is really broaden and combines many diverse aspects, such as market
research, product development, strategies to create user experiences for products
and services. All these disciplines are constantly evolving and are more and more
interconnected, leading to the creation of more complex and articulated models.

As an example, Envis Precisely (envis-precisely.com), a renowned studio for interaction design, proposes the overview of UX design shown in Fig. 2.3, which has been
inspired by the Dan Suffer's one [7].

According to this overview, there is a group of main disciplines that form the UX
Design: *Information Architecture, Communication Design, Motion Design* and *Interaction Design*. Some other disciplines share different aspects of the UX Design, yet
not being included in its totality, which are: *Architecture, Industrial Design, Human
Factors & Ergonomics,* and *Computer Science.* Although all these disciplines seem
separate, they still overlap a great deal. In fact, where the disciplines overlap there
can be major areas of practice, such as *User Interface Design*, where *Communication Design* and *Interaction Design* meet; or Data & Information Visualisation where
Communication Design and Computer Science meet Information Architecture.

Interestingly, a wide area in this overview is taken by the *Interaction Design*, that
is the design of interactive products and services in which the focus of designers
goes beyond the item being developed to incorporate the way users will interact with
them [8], which includes many aspects from different disciplines.

2.1 The UX Design Approach

The most valuable products and services, regardless of their industrial sector, have
the purpose of facing people's needs and solving people's problems. Keeping in mind
the UCD approach, UX design teams seek to understand *what* people need, *how* they

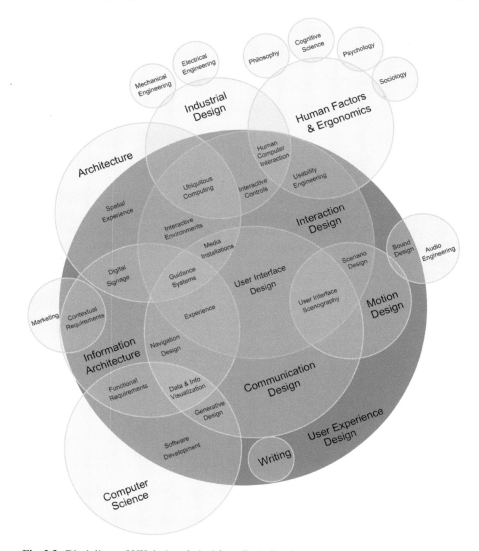

Fig. 2.3 Disciplines of UX design, forked from Envis Precisely (envis-precisely.com)

think, and *why* they act in a specific way with the aim of defining, understanding, and solving their problems in the best possible way.

The relation between the *what*, *how* and why has been developed by Simon Sinek in the Golden Circle [9], with the aim of understanding how companies and leaders are able to inspire people and be successful while others are not. The Golden Circle model is depicted in Fig. 2.4 and can be referenced to as a general UX Design approach.

Fig. 2.4 Golden circle
model proposed by Sinek [9]

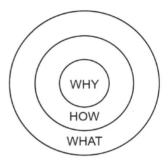

In the model, the *what* describes the things people can do with a product or a service. The *how* relates to the specific actions, strategies and methods needed to design a product. The *why* is the purpose of the product or service. In particular, the latter aspect refers to the users' motivations behind the selection of a specific product, the values, and views that users associate with that product, and also the identification of the needs and problems of the users to solve. Sinek states that "*People don't buy what you do, they buy why you do it.*" [9]. Thus, the *why* is probably the most important aspect to get and communicate. Consequently, UX designers should consider the *why* before determining the *what* and then, and finally, the *how* to create meaningful experiences.

However, identifying the users' motivations and needs can be challenging. A designer typically follows a specific methodology to design experience, particularly in complex design contexts. Most designers are familiar with "Design thinking" and adopt it as a UX Design process.

2.2   Design Thinking Model: Stages, Process, and Tools

Design thinking is an iterative process that design teams use to understand users, define and redefine problems and create innovative solutions to subsequently prototype and test. Many models have been proposed to define the Design thinking process. These models follow a similar process flow, and they vary mainly for the approach, number of stages and naming of each stage.

One of the most popular design thinking models is the one proposed by the *Hasso-Plattner Institute of Design at Stanford (d.school)* [10]. The aim of this model is to create practical and logical innovation, focusing on solving problems and finding possible solutions. This model includes five stages: *empathize, define, ideate, prototype,* and *test* (Fig. 2.5). The model describes a process that is non-linear and iterative. In fact, the stages are not strictly sequential, and are adaptable, repeatable, and cyclical.

A set of specific tools is associated with each of these stages, which the designers can use to frame the strategy and organise the project. Some of these tools are those

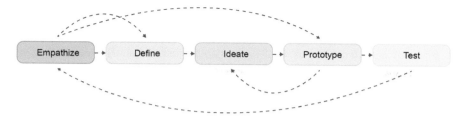

Fig. 2.5 Design thinking stages of the Hasso-Plattner Institute of Design at Stanford model [10]

commonly used in the UCD. In fact, the design thinking model adopts an approach that is user centred.

Empathize is the starting point of the design process. Initially, it is extremely important to have an empathic understanding of the problems that the product or service are expected to solve. Therefore, the focus is on the users' motivations and needs. This stage can be intended as the *why* of the Golden Circle that was mentioned above. At this stage in the process, it is strategic to formulate questions, by adopting the users' point of view. Designers are encouraged to cast aside all the assumptions and to objectively consider all possibilities. Fundamental is observing the users while performing tasks in a specific context and taking notes about their behaviours, to lately find patterns across seemingly diverse groups of people. This is where some methods are effectively used to collect information, and when experts from different disciplines are involved. The most common methods and research tools used in the Empathize stage are the following:

- *shadowing* consists in observing how people accomplish certain tasks in the environment, without influencing them. It is a qualitative research tool that allows designers to understand implicit users' behaviors and motivations.
- *interviews* help designers collecting information by directly communicating with the users or stakeholders. There are different types of interviews that can be used according to the specific goal. With directed interviews designers ask specific questions presenting a typical question-and-answer structure. Conversely, non-directed interviews allow designers to open a conversation about the topic to explore, and it is typically carried out setting up guidelines to convey the conversation and to collect valuable information.
- *surveys and questionnaires* are generally used to gather a large amount of information. These methods are delivered anonymously, allowing the users to freely express their point of view about a product or service.

To group and consolidate the information collected so far, designers can use different tools and maps. Some of these are storytelling tools that allow them to create empathy with users throughout the whole design process. Hereafter, there is a list of the most popular research tools:

- *personas* can be created to identify the target users and analyse them adopting their point of view. Personas underline the target demographics, behaviors, needs, and motivations through the creation of a fictional character.
- *scenario* are stories created to understand user's background, motivations, challenges, environment, and context of use.
- *empathy map* is a tool used to collect evaluations on the perceptions and feelings of the user. It generally represents a group of users, such as a customer segment.
- *list of user feedbacks* is created by extracting a list of keywords from interviews, surveys and questionnaires that help in classifying and understanding better the problems to address.

The main output of the Empathize phase is the list of the users' needs and of the product requirements.

In the **Define** phase, the data collected in the previous stage are analysed, synthesised, and organised to define the core problems. A *list of needs* is created, including a classification and relevance of the needs to address. There are numerous categories of user needs that must be addressed, and a selection of these is presented in Table 2.1.

Table 2.1 Types of user's needs

Types of user's needs	Description
Functions	Things that a user needs to accomplish with the product
Features	How product functions are implemented
Performance	Capacity of the product to fulfil the requirements
Efficiency	A need to use resources efficiently
Comfort	Sense of physical or psychological ease when using the product
Learnability	Intuitive user interface, so that the product can be used without training
Accessibility	Needs of user with diverse characteristics and abilities
Customization	Product can be personalised to meet user's preferences
Aesthetic appeal	Product is aesthetically pleasing
Multisensory experience	User can experience the product through multiple senses (vision, touch, hearing, smell, taste)
Reliability	Product performs consistently
Durability	Product resists and does not break
Reusability	Ability to reuse the product
Maintainability	Product is easy to maintain
Safety	Risks related to the use of product are zero or low

Also, in this stage there are research tools that help designers to interpret and sort the data out:

- *focus group* has the aim to find out different attitudes and responses about a topic. It consists in the organization of a selected group of users that discuss about a product, service, concept, or idea, in a comfortable environment. In the organization of a focus group, the presence of a moderator (facilitator) is fundamental to keep the discussion on track.
- *workshop* where team members can debate about a topic or a problem together, by going through a series of group exercises designed to get to a specific outcome. In this phase, it is practice discussing about the items of information collected and selecting the most important ones.

Moreover, maps are often used in this stage as an analysis tool:

- *experience map* represents the entire experience of a general user, without any reference to specific products or services. This map is used to create a baseline to understand the general human perspective.
- *customer journey map* is the most common map used in the design process, which provides a picture of the User Experience organized according to its main steps. Through this map the designer underlines the pain points, the user feelings and thoughts framing the users' motivations and needs in each step of the journey.
- *service blueprint map* is a representation of the entire process of service delivery representing the flow of actions that each actor needs to perform along the process. It allows designers to highlight the actions that the user can see and the ones that happen in the backstage, identifying everything that happens under the surface.

Usually, the development of these three maps is sequential: at first designers create the experience map and then the customer journey map, and eventually they proceed with the generation of the service blueprint map.

The main output of the Define phase consists in the creation of the *design brief*, hence the definition of the goals and deliverables of the project, articulating the desired results, the businesses and organisations needed.

Ideate. At this point of the design process, after the first research and analysis, the designers know the users' needs and motivations, the problems they are facing, the pain points to solve and the meaning the users are looking for. This is the moment for the generation of ideas and concepts that give an answer to the list of needs defined in the previous stage. These solutions are usually created keeping in mind the *design brief* and the *desirability* (what people desire), *feasibility* (what is feasible in terms of technical, engineering, organizational aspects) and *viability* (what is viable focusing on the business structure) goals.

Nonetheless, in this phase it is essential to propose as many creative ideas as possible, and to collect innovative results to the problems previously defined. It is common that many of the proposed ideas are not feasible or realistic. However, it is important to express them without prevention and judgment in a free-thinking environment, to stimulate the discussion between the team members. In fact, sharing thoughts and impressions at many levels is the key to stimulate creativity.

At the end of this collaborative activity, the ideas can be analysed and selected with the aim to keep the most valuable ones. Moreover, it is in this phase that is generated a collaborative dialogue between all the involved stakeholders, to understand their specific motivations, potentials, and constraints.

Also, it is at this time that aspects such as *usability, affordance, accessibility,* and *aesthetics* are considered. There is a wide variety of techniques for idea generation that can help designers during this Ideate stage. Some of them are the following:

- *brainstorming* is an effective method that starts from the problems previously defined to generate a wide range of ideas. The approach to adopt is a free-thinking one, in which people need to express themselves without filters, in a positive environment with no judgments. Sometimes, the most bizarre ideas can stimulate a constructive discussion, leading to innovative solutions.
- *benchmark* is when designers make comparisons with competitors, considering the design industry or a stakeholder-determined goal. It consists in evaluating products or services performances by using metrics. Benchmark also allows designers to set the context for the project development, that is defined considering the many different aspects previously analysed.

Once generated, the ideas must be well organized and represented, which is typically done using maps and sketches:

- *mind map* allows designers to organise and locate the information visually, to create a systematic and meaningful structure. It is generally formed by the central topic, which is placed in the middle, and its associated subtopics around it. This technique is useful to build an intuitive framework around a central concept. An example of mind map can be found in Fig. 2.6.
- *concept map* allows designers to visualise complex topics and subtopics, that are interconnected in many ways. It is like a mind map, but here the focus is on the relationships between topics.
- *sketching* is used to represent ideas to be shared with the other member of the team. The purpose is not to create aesthetically pleasant drawings but to generate a wide range of solutions, making thoughts understandable for the others. Usually, arrows and annotations can help in this goal.

Prototype. This phase is considered as the core of the design thinking as it presents a transformation of designers' ideas into model solutions, in preparation for the testing phase. The creation of prototypes enables the design team to explore design options, determine different parameters, finalize the characteristics of the product.

A prototype is an early representation of a product built to analyse a concept and subsequently to test it. It can have different characteristics, being for example partially or totally functional, low or high fidelity. Different tools can be used during

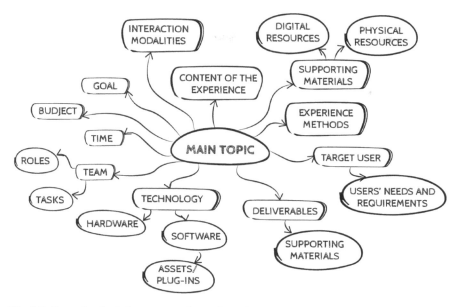

Fig. 2.6 Example of mind map presenting main topic and related sub-topics

this stage. A quick overview of the tools is given below, while a more in-depth discussion is provided in the next chapter:

- *storyboard* is a helpful tool to represent the solutions and to visualise the user interactions. It allows designers to create a story about the users' experience, framing the users' actions in the context of use.
- *3D model* is mainly used to represent physical products. It is a 3D representation that offers a clear view of how the design should look like and gives an idea of the final artifact. It is extremely useful to represent, analyse and understand the product architecture, components, mechanisms and how they are connected with each other. Moreover, starting from 3D models, designers can also create realistic renderings to show the product aesthetics, that is called the "look".
- *wireframe* is mainly used for the design of digital products as apps and websites. It provides a basic overview of the product, establishing the internal structure and interactions. Through wireframes, designers define the correct position of contents and functionalities. High-fidelity wireframes can be used as a starting point to create virtual prototypes. An illustration of a wireframe for a digital product application is depicted in Fig. 2.7 as an example.
- *physical prototype* is a tangible representation of the final product. It allows designers to experience many product characteristics, including aesthetics and ergonomics. There are many types of physical prototypes, which are developed

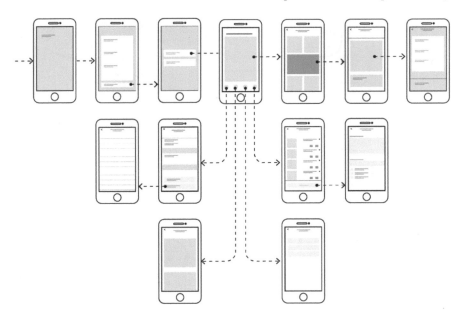

Fig. 2.7 Example of application wireframe related to a digital product

with different aims. As an example, a physical prototype can be a proof-of-principle one, a working one, a visual prototype, a functional one or a paper one.

- *virtual prototype* is a digital model, sometimes called digital mock-up, that simulates the physical product and is built to analyse and test its behaviours under real world operating conditions. The computer simulations can be enhanced using a variety of technologies, such as eXtended Reality technologies.

Test. After preparing a prototype, it is necessary to test it to gather information and valuable feedback about the interaction with real users, possibly in real use contexts. This stage allows designers to understand what the key features of the product are and what still needs to be improved, identifying for example usability, affordance, or accessibility issues. At this stage it is important to evaluate how the users perceive the product and how they interact with it, to determine whether the product meets the target, before taking it to the market. Prior to experimenting with any test, it is fundamental to establish the metrics against which the characteristics and performance will be measured. Usually, the result of these activities consists in a list of user feedback, evaluations, and proposed refinements. At this stage it is possible to use different testing techniques. Some of them are:

- *usability test*, which consists in observing a user interacting with the prototype or the product, with the purpose of determining its usability. During the test, in most of the cases, a researcher acts as facilitator, asking the user to complete a set of open or specific tasks. In the meanwhile, a second researcher takes notes on the user behaviors. The most used types of usability tests are *moderated, unmoderated,* and *guerrilla tests*. These three types of usability tests exhibit minor variations. In moderated tests, a facilitator or moderator follows a pre-prepared script to conduct the testing and directly poses qualitative questions to the participants. On the other hand, unmoderated tests require participants to carry out the testing independently without any moderation. This approach enables the organization of multiple tests and the rapid collection of a significant amount of data. Typically, the data collected during unmoderated tests are quantitative in nature. Guerrilla tests, on the other hand, are characterized by quick and cost-effective usability tests where qualitative data is typically gathered. The distinct feature of guerrilla tests is that participants are recruited on the spot in public spaces, such as shops or cafés, without prior contact.

- *A/B test*, which is carried out by administering to users' different options (the test name itself recalls two versions, A and B) and collecting their impressions. This test is used to evaluate different variants of the same concept, with the purpose of understanding which of the two versions is more performing and acceptable by the users. It is helpful when designers are struggling to choose between two solutions.

Table 2.2 provides an overview of the stages of the *Design Thinking* model that have been described above, where the objective, the tools for data collection and analysis and the output are collected and summarised for each stage.

Table 2.2 Overview of the stages, tools, and output of the design thinking model

Stage	Emphatize	Define	Ideate	Prototype	Test
Objective	Detect user's motivations and needs	Define core problems and list of needs	Generate ideas and concepts to meet users' needs	Transform ideas into model solutions to explore design options	Get feedback from the users and determine if the product meets the requirements
Tools for data collection	Shadowing • Interviews • Surveys and questionnaires	• Focus group • Workshop	• Brainstorming • Benchmark		
Tools for analysis and representation	• Personas • Scenarios • Empathy maps • List of user feedback	• Experience map • Customer journey map • Service blueprint map	• Mind map • Concept map • Sketching	• Storyboard • 3D model • Wireframe • Physical prototype • Virtual prototype	• Usability tests • A/B test
Output	Users' needs	Design brief	Concepts	Product models and prototypes	Users' feedback and proposed design refinements

As mentioned before, the *Design Thinking* process flow is never unidirectional, and although there is an order, the experimental, exploratory approach is applied to iterate among the phases. Some of the tools that have been mentioned in the various stages of the design process are not strictly linked to that stage, but can be used in other moments as well, according to the design aspects to explore. For example, the research and analysis will be slightly different depending on whether it concerns the design of new products, services and systems or if it is about the design to update the user experience for existing products, services and systems. In each of these cases, a suitable research strategy must be employed in the investigation of the User Experience.

2.3 Other Design Models

Nowadays, UX designers use other more recent models, which have a foundation on the model proposed by the *Hasso-Plattner Institute of Design at Stanford (d.school)* [10]. As examples we mention the ZURB Design Thinking model [11] or the IBM Design Thinking Process [12].

Another design model often used by UX designers is the *Double Diamond model* that was proposed by the British Design Council [13]. Even if this model organizes the design activities into four phases, these phases and the associated tools find some correspondence with those included in the Design Thinking model, which have been discussed above. The Double Diamond model consists of the following four phases: *discover, define, develop,* and *deliver* (Fig. 2.8).

In the *discover* phase, information is collected to understand the users, their motivations and needs. *Define* means filtering through all the information into a problem definition. During the *develop* phase, many ideas are explored to reach the problem

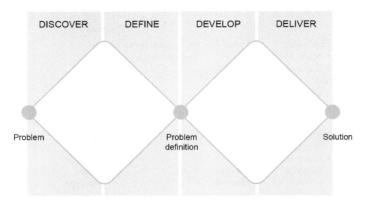

Fig. 2.8 Double diamond model proposed by the British Design Council [13]

solutions. Finally, the *deliver* phase consists of choosing the best solution, testing, and launching it to the market.

In these four phases, divergent thinking (in which the design team is open to many new ideas) and convergent thinking (where the design team focuses only on a few ideas trying to identify the most innovative solutions) are alternated, ideally following the two diamonds.

The first two phases, discover and define, represent the area dedicated to research, while the last two ones, develop and deliver, are dedicated to design.

The same basic principles that we have seen applied in the Design Thinking process are also adopted in the Double Diamond process and can be summarised as follows: user-first, iterate, collaborate, and co-create. A substantial difference concerns the prototype and test phases of the first model, which are merged into a single phase in the Double Diamond model, i.e., the deliver phase.

2.4   User Experience and Digital Products

Nowadays, design is rapidly expanding its focus by addressing immaterial artefacts and digital solutions besides material products. In this new context, the role of the UX designer may be mistakenly seen as a person that just design interfaces for digital products, excluding the tangible sphere of the interaction. In fact, more and more the role of UX design is associated with the mere creation of websites or applications. This conception is also exasperated by some professional training courses where design and prototyping software tools such as Sketch [14], Figma [15], Adobe XD [16], Principle [17] are often recommended as the main tools that a practitioner should learn to become a UX designer.

Especially online courses and blogs are shifting the educational assets for UX designers, pushing their role exclusively towards the design of digital products, which is also influenced by the kind of tools, which are closer to communication, branding and motion graphics. Moreover, many online articles dealing with topics of UX Design focus on those aspects that exclusively concern the digital features of products, completely neglecting topics such as the tangible interaction, product usability and affordance, or physical prototyping. Sometimes, companies associate the role of the UX designer with the design of apps and websites, subtracting it from its broader meaning. Furthermore, the figure of the UX designer is often linked and sometimes even mistakenly confused with that of the User Interface (UI) designer. In the collective imagination this led to the creation of hybrid figures, the so-called UX/UI designers.

Recalling the scheme of the Disciplines of UX Design [7] shown in Fig. 2.3, we notice that User Interface Design is classified as a subset of the broader User Experience Design domain and that the two cannot be considered equivalent. To clarify, the UI Design refers to the actual interface of the product, its visual representation, and its interactive elements. The UI designer deals with the look, the feel and the interactivity of a digital product. Instead, the UX designer adopts a wider view, considering the whole users' journey to solve a problem.

However, there is an increasing identification in UX designers as those who create user interfaces. Besides, the effort in the activities and guidelines that are necessary to design an effective UX for successful digital products is growing as well. As an example, Yablonski in Laws of UX [18] tries to make complex psychology heuristics and principles more accessible to designers in the creation of user interfaces (Table 2.3).

The guidelines established by Yablonski aim to make psychological heuristics that are pertinent to the user experience more accessible to designers [18]. Heuristics can be described as mental shortcuts or rules-of-thumb that aid in decision-making. Specifically, the Laws of UX identify seven heuristics, which are as follows:

- The Aesthetic-Usability Effect suggests that designs that are aesthetically pleasing are perceived as more usable.
- Fitts's Law states that the time required to reach a target is dependent on the distance to the target and its size.
- The Goal-Gradient Effect describes the phenomenon where the tendency to approach a goal increases as the individual gets closer to achieving it.
- Hick's Law relates to the time it takes to make a decision, which increases based on the number and complexity of available choices.
- Jakob's Law states that users transfer their expectations and familiarity with one product to other products that appear similar.
- Miller's Law pertains to the limited capacity of the average person's working memory, which is typically around 7 ($\pm$ 2) pieces of information.
- Parkinson's Law suggests that work expands to fill the available time allocated to complete it.

Table 2.3 Laws of UX for user interfaces design, collected by Yablonski [18]

Heuristic	Principle	Gestalt	Cognitive bias
Aesthetic-usability effect	Doherty threshold	Law of common region	Peak-end rule
Fitts's law	Postel's law	Law of proximity	Serial position effect
Goal-gradient effect	Tesler's law	Law of Pragnanz	Von Restorff effect
Hick's law	Occam's Razor	Law of similarity	Zeigarnik effect
Jakob's law	Pareto principle	Law of uniform connectedness	
Miller's law			
Parkinson's law			

Yablonski also describes five Principles, considered as fundamental rules:

- The Doherty Threshold refers to the point at which the responsiveness of an interaction reaches a level that feels real-time.
- *Postel's Law* advises to "be liberal in what you accept from others, and conservative in what you do."
- *Tesler's Law*, also known as the law of conservation, states that there is a certain level of complexity inherent in any system that cannot be reduced.
- *Occam's Razor*, or the law of parsimony, suggests that among competing hypotheses that make equally accurate predictions, the one with the fewest assumptions should be favored.
- The *Pareto Principle* posits that roughly 80% of effects come from 20% of causes, meaning that a minority of inputs or factors contribute to the majority of outcomes.

The Gestalt psychological approach centers around the perception of reality and the understanding of various phenomena. Yablonski outlines five key Gestalt Laws of UX:

- the *Law of Common Region*, also known as the Law of Grouping, suggests that elements within a defined boundary tend to be perceived as a group;
- the *Law of Proximity* states that objects that are close to each other are perceived as belonging to the same group;
- the *Law of Prägnanz* emphasizes that complex images or designs are simplified and perceived in the simplest form possible to reduce cognitive effort;
- the *Law of Similarity* suggests that elements with similar characteristics, such as shape, color, or size, are perceived as belonging together or forming a group;
- the *Law of Uniform Connectedness* states that elements that are visually connected or linked are perceived as more related than elements without any connection.

Regarding cognitive bias, which refers to the unconscious deviation from rational judgment or decision-making, Yablonski outlines four guidelines:

- the *Peak-End Rule* suggests that the overall evaluation of an experience is primarily influenced by the feelings experienced at its peak and at its end, rather than considering the total sum or average of every moment;
- the *Serial Position Effect* indicates that people tend to remember the first and last items in a series more easily than the items in the middle;
- the *Von Restorff Effect*, also known as the isolation effect, states that among multiple similar objects, the one that stands out or differs from the others is more likely to be remembered;
- the *Zeigarnik Effect* predicts that uncompleted or interrupted tasks are better remembered than completed ones.

Considering these guidelines, it is possible to notice that they take up general bases and that many of them are applicable to the design of physical products and not only to the design of digital artifacts. This makes it clear how the role of the UX designer cannot be strictly related to a specific field or technology. Indeed, the final goal is the creation of a meaningful user experience, beyond the technology used.

The different UX processes can be applied to various fields, for the resolution of problems of different levels and for proposing innovative solutions. More and more, the design of memorable experiences involves a multiplicity of aspects, especially to create a deep involvement of the user and to elicit an emotional response.

To this end, technology is increasingly being used to create immersive, interactive, and multisensory solutions that engage the user on the subjective and personal level, arousing emotions and feelings.

References

1. ISO 9241-210 (2010) International Organization for Standardization. Ergonomics of human-system interaction—Part 210: human-centered design for interactive systems (formerly known as 13407)
2. Newbery P, Farnham K (2013) Experience design: a framework for integrating brand, experience, and value. Wiley
3. Norman D, Nielsen J (2021) The definition of user experience (UX). Nielsen Norman Group. https://www.nngroup.com/articles/definition-user-experience/. Last accessed 15 May 2023
4. Norman D (2017) The design of everyday things: revised and expanded edition. MIT Press
5. Interaction Design Foundation, UCD: https://www.interaction-design.org/literature/topics/user-centered-design. Last accessed 15 May 2023
6. Mesut J (2023) Shaping design, designers and teams, DesignOps summit 2018. https://www.slideshare.net/RosenfeldMedia/shaping-designers-and-design-teams-jason-mesut-at-design ops-summit-2018. Last accessed 15 May 2023
7. Saffer D (2009) Designing for interaction: creating innovative applications and devices, 2nd edn. New Riders
8. Interaction Design Foundation, HCI: https://www.interaction-design.org/literature/topics/human-computer-interaction. Last accessed 15 May 2023
9. Sinek S (2009) Start with why: how great leaders inspire everyone to take action. Penguin
10. Hasso P, Meinel C, Ulrich Weinberg U (2009) Design-thinking. Mi-Fachverlag, Landsberg am Lech
11. ZURB. https://zurb.com. Last accessed 15 May 2023
12. Percival L, Braz A, Chicoria A, Tizzei L (2016) IBM design thinking software development framework. In: Brazilian workshop on agile methods processings. Springer
13. Eleven lessons: managing design in eleven global companies—desk research report. Design Council, 2007, https://dokumen.tips/documents/eleven-lessons-managing-design-in-eleven-global-companies-2015-03-23-eleven-lessons.html?page=1. Last access 15 May 2023
14. Sketch. https://www.sketch.com/. Last accessed 15 May 2023
15. Figma. https://www.figma.com/. Last accessed 15 May 2023
16. Adobe XD. https://www.adobe.com/it/products/xd.html. Last accessed 15 May 2023
17. Principle. https://principleformac.com/. Last accessed 15 May 2023
18. Yablonski J (2020) Laws of UX: using psychology to design better products & services. O'Reilly Media

Chapter 3
Prototyping: Practices and Techniques

Abstract This chapter discusses the complex process of introducing new products to the market and the challenges involved. It highlights the importance of understanding user needs, both explicit and latent, in order to create products that meet customer requirements and provide a positive user experience. Failure to properly analyze user needs can lead to product dissatisfaction and costly design changes later in the process. The chapter emphasizes key requirements for new products, including style, functionality, quality, safety, and sustainability, and also explores the cost of design changes and the significance of addressing design problems early in the development process. It explains how the cost of fixing issues increases as the product development progresses and emphasizes the importance of timely validation and testing to minimize the cost impact of changes. Prototyping is identified as a valuable tool in the product development process for evaluating user needs and refining design concepts. It explains the iterative nature of prototyping and its role in eliminating unfeasible or undesirable solutions. The chapter discusses the purposes of prototypes, such as experimentation, learning, communication, testing, exploration, education, and research. Different types and scopes of prototypes are explained, including comprehensive and focused prototypes, as well as the concept of fidelity, which measures the degree of resemblance between the prototype and the final product. The chapter also provides an overview of various prototyping resources, such as sketches, wireframes, physical models, 2D and 3D renderings, interactive prototyping, and virtual prototyping using eXtended Reality technologies.

Introducing new products to the market is a complex process that involves a significant investment of time and money. Despite this, not all product launches are successful [1]. Some examples are the Google Glass, a wearable computer released in 2013 but discontinued due to privacy and usability concerns, and the Amazon Fire Phone, a smartphone released in 2014 but discontinued due to low sales.

Introducing new products is a challenging task, as the market demands complex products with fewer design flaws. The pressure to create unique and differentiated products is high, but this becomes even harder when resources are limited. The time-to-market is also a factor, as a longer design process is necessary to ensure high-quality products, but this conflicts with the need for a speedy launch.

In the development of a new product, designers create solutions to meet identified requirements, which may stem from a market analysis of user needs or from the technical department and must be met by the design concepts. The collection and understanding of user needs is crucial in the early stages of new product development. This involves setting requirements based on both explicit and latent needs, which can add value to the product. Explicit needs are directly stated by the customer, while latent needs are underlying, implicit, and often unarticulated needs that a customer may not be aware of. For instance, an explicit need is the desire for a coffee machine that can make multiple cups of coffee at once, latent need is that the coffee machine can also make tea, hot chocolate, and other beverages. Product designers need to understand both explicit and latent needs to create products that effectively meet customer requirements and provide a positive user experience.

If user needs are not properly analyzed, there is a risk that the product may not meet expectations and changes may have to be made later in the process, potentially leading to difficulties in integrating them into the design. As an example, let's say a company is developing a new smartwatch. The company sets requirements based on both explicit and latent needs by conducting surveys, focus groups, and in-depth interviews with potential users. Through these methods, they discover that users value long battery life, waterproof capabilities, and stylish design. However, they also uncover latent needs such as the need for a heart rate monitor, GPS tracking, and the ability to receive notifications from their smartphone. By taking these needs into account, the company can add value to the product and make sure it meets the expectations of users. Conversely, if the company had not properly analyzed user needs, they may have only focused on long battery life and waterproof capabilities, leading to a product that does not meet the needs and expectations of users. The company would then have to make changes later in the process, potentially leading to difficulties and costs in integrating them into the design.

3.1 Key Requirements for New Products

In addition to user needs, product requirements encompass all necessary functions, features, and behaviors for the product to be efficient, user-friendly, safe, and cost-effective. The following is a summary of key requirements for a new product.

Style. Style refers to a group of similar product designs. In the development of new products and services, form, and design, in general, are considered increasingly important. The form of a product can impact customer perception and understanding of its value [2]. Many well-known brands have products that are recognizable by their style. Examples of brands with iconic styles are Apple with its minimalist and clean design for its smartphones, laptops, and other devices; Louis Vuitton with its signature monogram design on its luxury handbags and accessories; and Harley-Davidson with its recognizable motorcycles with loud engines and bold design elements.

Functionality. Every product is developed with specific goals in mind. For instance, bicycles are designed to transport people to their destinations through

cycling, with specific technical features like gears or batteries. The functional requirements of a product encompass all these technical details. Among the functionalities
of a product, reliability is especially important and can be measured in terms of time
until failure and likelihood of failure.

Usability and User Experience. Usability refers to a product's ease of use, intu-
itiveness, and learnability. The ISO 9241-11 standard developed by the International Organization for Standardization (ISO) outlines this definition of usability:
"the extent to which a product, system or service can be used by specified users to
achieve specified goals with effectiveness, efficiency and satisfaction in a specified
context of use" [3]. Usability is crucial for all products that involve human-technology
or human–machine interaction. A product with good usability often goes unnoticed,
whereas poor usability can lead to frustration for users. The concept of usability refers
to a product's ease of use and includes factors such as intuitive navigation in an app
and quick learning. Usability is considered a subfield of the larger concept of *user
experience*, which encompasses a user's overall perception and emotions related to
using a product. User experience considers not only the effectiveness and efficiency
of using a product, but also the enjoyment and satisfaction a user feels while using it.
ISO 9241-210 defines user experience as "person's perceptions and responses that
result from the use and/or anticipated use of a product, system or service." [3]. It
takes a comprehensive approach to evaluating the full experience of using a product,
with the aim of ensuring that users not only achieve their goals effectively, but also
experience positive emotions like joy and comfort.

Quality. Quality of products refers to features or elements that enhance the value
of a product beyond its functionality and features. It encompasses the value a product
holds for customers, its ability to fulfill its intended purpose, and its conformity to
established specifications. The typical quality requirements include user experience,
appearance, look and feel, materials, longevity, performance, maintainability, and
more. For example, the quality of a smartwatch is essential for customer satisfaction
and brand reputation. In addition to its basic features such as tracking fitness activities,
receiving notifications, and making calls, a quality smartwatch should also offer an
excellent user experience, with an easy-to-use interface, responsive touch screen,
and intuitive controls. Appearance is also important, with stylish designs that match
the latest fashion trends.

Safety. Safety in products refers to the potential for harm or injury to users when
using the product or service. It involves evaluating the potential dangers associated
with the product in real-world conditions. There are established safety standards and
regulations that provide guidelines and tests to ensure the safety of a product. Safety
requirements aim to minimize or eliminate potential risks, such as ensuring the well-
being, health, and protection of the users. For example, a quality smartwatch should be
safe for users to wear and use without risking any harm or injury. Safety requirements
for smartwatches include protection against electric shocks, heat, radiation, and other
potential hazards.

Sustainability. Sustainability is a growing concern for consumers and businesses
alike and is becoming an increasingly important factor in product design. Sustainability refers to the ability of a product or system to meet the needs of the present

without compromising the ability of future generations to meet their own needs. In the context of product design, sustainability is about creating products that are environmentally friendly, socially responsible, and economically viable. This can include reducing waste, conserving resources, reducing the carbon footprint of a product, and using materials that are safe and biodegradable. For instance, a sustainable product design might use renewable materials such as bamboo, cork, or recycled plastic, or incorporate features that help reduce the product's overall environmental impact, such as water-saving technology in household appliances. Incorporating sustainability into product design can lead to benefits for both the environment and the bottom line. It can help companies differentiate themselves from competitors and build a positive brand image, while also reducing costs associated with waste and environmental degradation. At the same time, it can help to protect the environment for future generations and create a better world for everyone.

3.2   The Cost of Design Changes

It is common for design teams to encounter challenges while developing a new product. There is a possibility that the proposed solution by the team may not fully meet the established requirements or may not be the best option from the start. Additionally, issues and uncertainties can arise during the product development stage.

The cost of fixing design problems increases as the development of a product progresses, as more time, money and resources have been invested, which makes fixing issues later in the process more expensive. Imagine a company developing a new smartwatch. During the initial design phase, the team realizes that the battery life is not as long as they had hoped. If they address this issue at this stage, it may take a few revisions to the design and some extra time and resources, but overall, it will be relatively inexpensive to fix. However, if the issue is not addressed until later in the development process, such as during the production phase, the costs can rapidly escalate. The tooling used to manufacture the watch may need to be modified, which can be expensive and time-consuming. The production schedule may need to be adjusted, potentially delaying the launch date, and losing potential sales. This example highlights how fixing design problems early in the process is much more cost-effective than fixing them later.

Therefore, it is essential to identify and make necessary changes in the product design at an early stage to minimize the cost impact of those changes. Changes that improve the user experience, increase the company's ability to sell the product, or reduce the cost of production are typically valuable and worth making.

The cost of change curve, illustrated in Fig. 3.1, demonstrates how the cost of correcting mistakes rises rapidly as they are detected later in the product development process. The graph illustrates that changes made early in the project's execution stage can result in added value. However, beyond that point, changes tend to become increasingly detrimental to the project, with cost rising and opportunity and value decreasing. This is due to the extensive re-design and re-testing required.

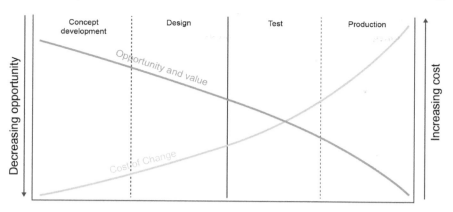

Fig. 3.1 Cost of design changes and opportunity to add value

Minimizing the costs of necessary changes can be achieved by conducting frequent and early testing. Timeliness in validating and testing design concepts is crucial in making informed decisions and reducing the overall cost impact of changes.

3.3 Prototyping

The product development process typically consists of iterative activities that progress from the initial concept idea to the final production of the product. This process typically includes several stages, where the generation of the new product idea is tested, refined, and designed in detail before the production starts (Fig. 3.2).

The "Prototyping and Testing and Concept Refinement" phase of the product development process is critical for the design team. It allows for early testing and refinement of conceptual ideas, even if the design is not yet fully developed. During this stage, only a portion of the eventual features may be tested, but these tests play a crucial role in eliminating unfeasible or undesirable solutions and improving the

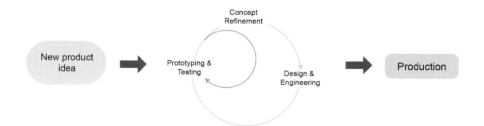

Fig. 3.2 Concept design and design and engineering testing loops

value of the product. By shortening the feedback loop, or the time between generating ideas and testing them, the cost of change can be significantly reduced.

Iterative design can also be carried out later when issues are encountered during the Design and Engineering phase. Each iteration provides the design team with the opportunity to gather more information and make improvements or modifications to the design. These changes aim to enhance the product but come with a cost whose extent depends on when the change request is made. If the cycle of prototyping, testing, and making changes is carried out early in the conceptual design phase, the cost of changes will be lower.

Prototyping is a valuable tool for evaluating users' needs in product development (Fig. 3.3). It allows the design team to gather early feedback, validate design concepts, and refine the product in response to users' needs, which leads to a better final product. According to a revised version of the Design Wheel [4], the first phase of the design process, called *Explore*, involves identifying the needs of the users. The *Create* phase follows, where the design team outlines solutions to meet these needs. The *Evaluate* phase then assesses how well these solutions align with the users' needs. This is an iterative process, where the phases may be repeated several times until the optimal design solution is reached. Once a consensus has been reached on the desired features of the new product, its design process can commence. Instead of the central "manage" phase, we propose substituting the *Prototype* phase as the focus of the design process. Indeed, Prototyping is key to developing good products and good user experiences.

Prototyping can be defined as the process of creating tangible representations of design ideas for various purposes, including tests and communication. This experimental technique is used by design teams to bring their concepts to life and explore various possibilities, and to share them with others and determine their value.

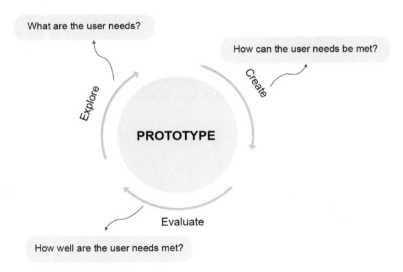

Fig. 3.3 Prototyping for user's needs evaluation

Prototyping is an essential part of gaining hands-on experience and knowledge in various design fields. It gives form to abstract concepts and makes them more understandable. It fosters collaboration and communication among researchers and practitioners by providing a tangible representation of ideas and solutions.

The word *prototype* has a specific meaning. Its roots come from:

- the Latin *proto*, which means origin, and
- *type* which means form or model.

Prototype is defined as "an approximation of the product along one or more dimensions of interest." [5]. The dimensions of interest are those listed in Sect. 3.1, and include style, functionality, usability, quality and performance, safety, and sustainability.

Prototypes are experimental model of an idea and serve as tangible representations that enable testing and refining of concepts. Evaluating design ideas and solutions involves creating a form that can be tested by both the design team and external users such as end-users and stakeholders. By utilizing prototypes, evaluation and testing can be pushed to the earlier stages of product design.

A prototype has various uses in the product development process, serving as a noun, verb, and adjective. For instance,

industrial designers create *prototypes* of their ideas,
engineers *prototype* their designs,
software developers write *prototype* programs.

In the realm of product development, prototypes serve as representations of product ideas. Typically, these models often highlight specific aspects relevant to their purpose, rather than encompassing all features and properties of the final product. As a result, prototypes can vary in their design and intended use, and these issues are depicted in Fig. 3.4 and explained in the rest of this chapter.

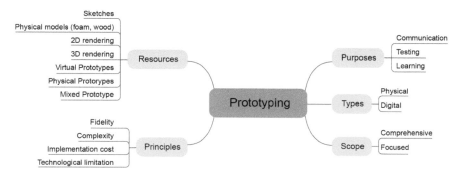

Fig. 3.4 Prototyping: purposes, types, scope, principles, and resources

3.4 Purposes of Prototypes

Prototyping is a critical aspect during the early stages of exploration, allowing for the shift from abstract to concrete through direct and tangible experience. Industrial designers can use prototyping to explore and envision new solutions, envision possible futures, delve into uncharted territories, and contribute to the design discourse with current concerns and hypothetical scenarios. Iteration through prototyping and testing enables designers to experiment with hundreds of design options and choose the most innovative product design.

Prototyping and user testing is the best way to make viable products that are impactful for users. By creating incrementally better prototypes throughout the design process, designers can get valuable feedback to improve the product. By using real people, and observing how they interact with prototypes, designers can identify precisely where they encounter difficulties, what they find confusing, and how they respond to the entire experience.

Creating a prototype involves replicating the essential elements of a product and serves as the foundation for its future development. The reasons for prototyping are multifaceted and include communication, testing, exploration, education, and research. Let's examine each of these purposes more closely.

Communication. It is crucial for the design team to effectively communicate their vision to stakeholders. Prototypes enrich communication with top management, marketing and extended team members, end users and customers, and investors.

The objective of communication is to transmit and exchange the general or specific aspects of a product concept. It is widely recognized that demonstrating an idea through an artifact is more valuable than solely discussing it. Designers can avoid the challenge of asking their audience to envision their idea by having a prototype, regardless of its level of fidelity. Merely describing their idea can lead to different interpretations by each individual, creating a mismatch of expectations. Prototypes enable designers to align everyone in the same direction, reducing the chances of miscommunication during the process, and provide a tangible representation that allows designers to clarify their ideas and bring everyone's perspective into alignment.

Testing. Testing and improving products are the main reason for prototyping. Various industries develop prototypes of their work to experiment with and assess different concepts. Testing is aimed at determining if the designed product aligns with the original requirements. This can be achieved by using a prototype to test design decisions and solutions with real users before development starts. The objective is to identify any issues or for improvement early on, allowing for necessary modifications to be made prior to development and ensuring that the final product meets user needs and expectations.

Iterative prototyping involves repeating the prototyping process to refine and improve the design (Fig. 3.5). Based on user feedback, the design team makes changes to the prototype and creates a new one, which is tested again. This cycle continues until the design meets the desired objectives and the users' needs. This

Fig. 3.5 Iterative prototyping in the design process

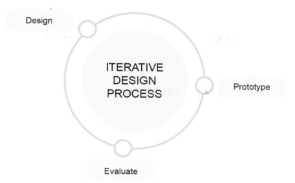

approach allows for a more thorough and informed design process, reducing the risk of creating a final product that does not meet the user's needs or expectations.

Experimentation and Learning. Prototypes can be used as tools for experimentation and learning, providing answers to questions about a product's features, functionality and quality. This information can be used to expand knowledge and enhance product characteristics and performance.

During the product development phase, problems and uncertainties can frequently arise. Exploring the issue through prototypes is an excellent method for the design team to understand the problem they are tackling and identify the best approach. Prototyping at this stage provides the design team with the freedom to explore multiple solutions to the problem, identify potential challenges that need to be addressed, and refine their ideas based on the feedback they receive.

Prototyping is not just limited to product development; it can also be used in educational settings to support learning. Prototyping can provide a hands-on, experiential learning experience for students, allowing them to engage with and explore concepts in a more tangible way. For example, students can create prototypes of a concept they are studying to gain a better understanding of how it works in practice. This can involve building physical models, creating digital simulations, or using other prototyping tools to explore different aspects of the concept. Prototyping can also be used in design thinking workshops and other educational settings to facilitate collaboration, creativity, and problem-solving. By working together to create prototypes, students can develop critical thinking skills, learn to collaborate effectively, and gain a deeper understanding of the design process.

3.5 Types, Scope and Principles of Prototypes

Prototyping converts theoretical concepts into tangible forms, giving designers a means to physically encounter their ideas that would otherwise remain only in their imaginations. "Experiencing" entails grasping ideas through the senses, and prototypes offer tangible representations that can be seen, heard, touched, and even smelled.

3.5.1 Types of Prototypes

Prototypes can take on tangible forms that are either physical or virtual (as shown in Fig. 3.6), and both forms enable us to encounter design ideas.

Physical prototypes are tangible objects designed to demonstrate specific aspects of a product. These traditional prototypes consist of actual objects that can be experienced physically through the senses, including vision, hearing, touch, and smell. A prototype can showcase a product's shape, color, material, functions, and user interface. Physical prototypes can be fully or partially functional and allow for the evaluation of the concept's sensory elements such as aesthetics and ergonomics. However, creating comprehensive physical prototypes may not always be practical due to factors such as complexity, cost, or resource consumption. For example, creating a full-scale, functioning prototype of a car with all its features, including engine, transmission, interior, and exterior design may be complex, costly, and resource-intensive. Therefore, more focused prototypes are developed to test specific requirements. For instance, creating a physical prototype of a car's steering wheel, designed

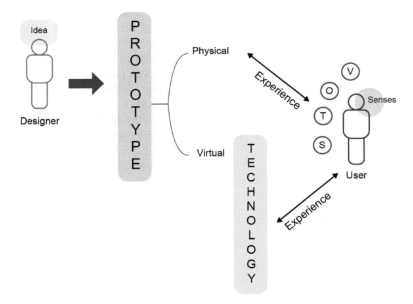

Fig. 3.6 Prototypes allow tangible representation of designers' ideas that can be perceived through senses (vision, hearing, touch, smell)

to test its usability and ergonomics may be less complex, less expensive, and less resource-intensive than a full-scale prototype.

One disadvantage of physical prototypes is that they are not easily modified, making iterations or modifications to the prototype complex, time-consuming, and expensive. An example could be a physical prototype of a new smartphone design. If the design team realizes that the placement of a particular button needs to be adjusted, they may need to create a new physical prototype from scratch to test the modified design. This can be a time-consuming and costly process, especially if the modifications require significant changes to the prototype.

Digital prototypes, also named virtual prototypes, refer to digital representations of a product, such as computer simulations and analytical models that can be analyzed and tested. These prototypes are technologically mediated representations of the product idea and allow for the experience of its properties. Advances in technology have greatly increased the capabilities of virtual prototyping in recent years. Examples of virtual prototypes include 3D geometry computer models and Virtual Reality-enhanced computer simulations. The advantage of virtual prototypes is their ease of modification, making testing and changes quicker and more flexible. However, some forms of testing, like tactile interaction, may not be fully possible due to the absence of physicality in the virtual prototype, which is a result of current limitations in technology.

3.5.2 Scopes of Prototypes

Prototyping can be classified as comprehensive or focused according to the scope and purpose of the prototyping effort.

A *comprehensive prototype* is a thorough depiction of the product, encompassing a majority of its characteristics. Such a prototype operates as a full-sized, fully functional version, capable of testing most of the specified requirements. For instance, fully functional prototypes of vehicles are considered comprehensive prototypes. They are created to resemble the final product as closely as possible and often possess almost all of the same attributes, such as design, functionality, and performance.

Focused prototypes highlight a single or a small number of specific features of a product. Employing multiple focused prototypes is a prevalent method to evaluate the overall performance. This enables the design team to obtain responses to their queries sooner than generating a comprehensive prototype. Two-dimensional renders or foam models serve as examples of focused prototypes used to examine a product's shape.

The decision to use a comprehensive or focused prototype depends on the stage of the design process and the specific goals of the prototype. A comprehensive prototype is useful in the early stages of product design when the goal is to explore and generate ideas. On the other hand, a focused prototype is used in later stages of design when the goal is to validate specific design decisions or test a particular feature or function of the product.

The degree of accuracy in developing a prototype, commonly referred to as "fidelity," is a critical aspect of prototyping. Fidelity pertains to the degree of resemblance between the prototype and the intended final product [6]. It may differ based on the requirements and objectives of the prototype, as well as the developmental stage of the product idea. The goal of user testing is to obtain comparable reactions from users towards the concept and the actual product. The degree of prototype fidelity can influence both the assessment of the design and the emotional responses of users.

As developing highly authentic prototypes can be expensive and time-consuming, the selection of the type of prototype will depend on the level of resemblance required for the final design. An instance of low-fidelity prototyping is the creation of rudimentary sketches utilizing basic tools like paper and colored pencils. Although low-fidelity prototypes may have restricted details, they serve as a cost-effective and uncomplicated means to convey the concept while still being impactful.

Fidelity measures the degree of similarity between the prototype and the desired final product, and several factors, such as the prototype's cost, complexity, and technological constraints, can impact it (as shown in Fig. 3.7), which are discussed in the following.

Low-fidelity prototypes are often used during the initial stages of the design process to explore and test out different concepts quickly and inexpensively. They are useful for rapidly generating and iterating ideas, as they require minimal time and resources to create. Low-fidelity prototypes can also be used to gather feedback from users early in the design process, which can inform further development of the product. Additionally, they can be used to test basic functionality and interactions, as well as to identify potential design flaws or usability issues. Low fidelity prototype is the easiest and cheapest prototype to make and does not require as much time or skill to complete. They help to make changes very quickly with little effort. Some examples include sketches, paper prototypes, wireframes, storyboards, mood boards and component prototypes. Figure 3.8 summarises when using low-fidelity prototypes.

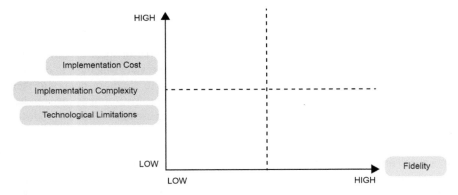

Fig. 3.7 Fidelity of prototypes versus implementation cost and complexity, and technological limitations

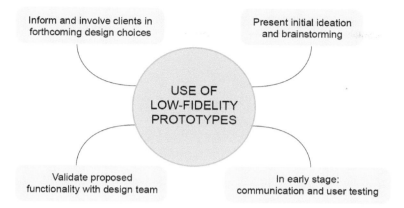

Inform and involve clients in forthcoming design choices

Present initial ideation and brainstorming

USE OF LOW-FIDELITY PROTOTYPES

Validate proposed functionality with design team

In early stage: communication and user testing

Fig. 3.8 Use of low-fidelity prototypes

High-fidelity prototypes are typically used in the later stages of the design process when the product's design has been largely finalized, and there is a need to test and refine its functionality and user experience. They are highly detailed and closely resemble the final product, making them suitable for assessing the product's performance and usability in real-world situations. High-fidelity prototypes can be useful for identifying potential design flaws or user experience issues that may have been missed during the low fidelity prototyping stage. Additionally, they can be utilized for user testing and feedback, enabling designers to make any necessary adjustments before the product's final release. However, the development of high-fidelity prototypes can be time-consuming and costly, making them more suitable for use in the later stages of the design process when the design has been largely finalized. Figure 3.9 provides an overview of when using high-fidelity prototypes.

As an example of use of low- and high-fidelity prototypes, a product design team is tasked with creating a new smartphone. They start by sketching out various design concepts and then create low-fidelity prototypes using cardboard or foam core to quickly test and refine their ideas. These prototypes might include rough representations of the phone's form, size, and functionality, but will not have all the details or functionality of a final product. Next, the team might create high-fidelity prototypes using 3D printing or other advanced technologies. These prototypes will be closer in appearance and functionality to the final product and can be used to test and validate design decisions. Finally, after several rounds of testing and refinement, the team will arrive at a final design that meets their goals for form, function, and target user.

Implementation costs. Physical prototyping is known to be a costly process, requiring significant investments in time and resources to produce detailed designs and prototype materials that are often discarded after the testing phase. Additionally, traditional production techniques for physical prototyping may require the creation of molds or programming of machine tools, further increasing the time and cost

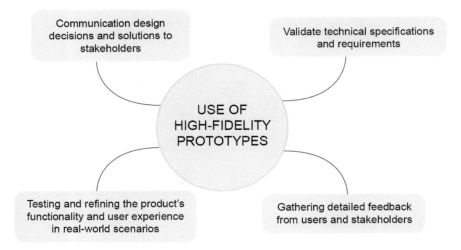

Fig. 3.9 Use of high-fidelity prototypes

required for development. Additive Manufacturing has helped to reduce the costs and development times associated with physical prototyping [7]. While the creation of virtual prototypes also incurs costs and development time, it is possible to optimize and reduce these through the reuse of software modules. However, despite these optimizations, the prototyping process may still require multiple iterations and physical prototypes due to design constraints, unexpected failures during testing, and potential errors in the manufacturing process.

Implementation complexity. The level of complexity involved in creating physical prototypes is dependent on the manufacturing technology used. Traditional manufacturing methods are typically more complex than newer technologies like Additive Manufacturing. Similarly, the complexity of virtual prototyping can vary depending on the software and hardware utilized. To make virtual prototyping more efficient and accessible, it is ideal to have a tool chain that is quick, easy to use, and has a low learning curve. In order to simplify the development process and reduce the required technical expertise, some software development platforms are available. For instance, 3D CAD software tools used by engineers and designers to create complex parts and assemblies help to reduce the complexity of the virtual prototyping process by offering intuitive interfaces and pre-built models.

Technological Limitation. The constraints in virtual prototyping primarily arise from the usage of eXtended Reality (XR) technology. Despite significant advancements in XR, it poses certain challenges in specific applications, especially in industrial environments. The challenges include the bulkiness and discomfort of headset devices, unintuitive Virtual Reality controllers, and limited haptic technology for various types of interactions. These factors can restrict the level of accuracy and realism that can be achieved in the prototypes developed.

3.6 Resources for Prototyping

There are various resources available for prototyping, depending on the specific product being developed and the level of fidelity required (as shown in Fig. 3.3). Here are some common resources used for prototyping.

Sketches and diagrams: These can be hand-drawn or created using digital tools and are useful for exploring early-stage ideas. Drawing sketches is a crucial component of the design process and can facilitate making important decisions about the designs. Sketches can range from basic, rough sketches on paper to more sophisticated, detailed sketches.

Wireframe is a preliminary representation of a product design in which the designer outlines the basic structure and layout of the product. It provides a general overview of an application or component, serving as the foundation of digital products. When designing an interactive application, such as an App, wireframes are created to clearly depict the layout of the app screen. Wireframes illustrate the intended placement of data and user interface elements, including buttons, tabs, icons, and drop-down menus, among others. The level of detail in wireframes can vary depending on the project requirements.

Physical models are often used early in the design process to help designers visualize and refine their ideas before moving on to more expensive and time-consuming prototyping methods. Physical models can be made using a variety of materials, including foam, wood, clay, plastic, and metal. To create these prototypes, skilled model makers are needed who possess expert manual dexterity in using tools such as chisels and cutters. The choice of material depends on the level of detail required, the durability needed, and the manufacturing process. Physical models can be used for both form studies (studying the visual appearance of a product) and functional studies (testing the usability and functionality of a product). Physical models can be scaled up or down in size depending on the requirements of the design. This allows designers to study the product from different perspectives and test its suitability for different user groups. Physical models can be used to test the ergonomics and functionality of a product design. For example, a product designer may create a physical model of a smartphone to show how it will fit in a user's hand.

2D rendering involves producing digital images that portray an object using raster graphics editors, such as Adobe Photoshop, with the goal of creating a realistic representation of a new product concept. 2D product renders are commonly used for communication, sales, marketing, and e-Commerce purposes. To create these digital images, designers may use a drawing tablet (also known as a graphic tablet) which functions as a computer input device and allows them to create product illustrations by hand using a stylus pen, mimicking the experience of drawing with pencil and paper.

3D digital model is a computer-generated mathematical representation of an object that is produced through the technique of 3D modeling in computer graphics. This process results in a digital representation of an object that can be fully animated and simulated, making it useful in various media. 3D modeling has become a widely used tool across various industries, including consumer product, automotive design, industrial equipment manufacturing, architecture, design, engineering, entertainment, gaming, and many others. Typically, Computer Aided Design (CAD) tools are used to create 3D digital representations of objects. The level of detail in a 3D model can vary and is often used in the design and engineering fields to depict products. The digital models can also be turned into static images through 3D rendering or technical drawings. The advantages of using 3D modeling include the ability to visualize the design's 3D form in a clear and easy manner, as well as the capacity to generate photo-realistic images that aid in the assessment of the product's appearance. In addition, the ability to automatically calculate physical properties such as mass and volume saves time and effort. By creating a single canonical description of the design, the process becomes more efficient, allowing for the creation of other descriptions such as cross-sectional views and fabrication drawings. 3D models can also be imported into other digital tools for simulations and animations. For example, Unity 3D development platform [8] can be used to create virtual environments, and Finite Element Analysis (FEA) software can be used to test product behavior under different conditions, including forces, vibrations, and heat. Besides, the digital models created through 3D modeling can be transformed into physical objects using traditional manufacturing processes or the modern 3D printing technology.

Interactive prototyping is a process of building an interactive experience that helps others understand a design vision. It is useful for pitching ideas, explaining design details, and usability testing. Interactive digital prototypes are working models that show how a final product would look and behave. They are often used for prototyping apps and can be created without coding using tools such as InVision, Adobe XD, Axure RP, Balsamiq, and JustInMind.

Physical prototypes are produced by creating one or more physical components that can be assembled. As previously discussed, basic physical prototypes can be made using various methods, including manual techniques that use pliable materials like plasticine, wood, or polystyrene. Instead of manual methods, physical prototypes can be created using traditional manufacturing techniques like machining, milling, or molding. This approach requires a detailed product design, a model or technical drawing, and planning the production process, which involves programming the machine or creating a mold. However, this method can be complex and time-consuming due to the need for a more detailed product description and the cost of setting up a production line. The utilization of modern technologies, such as 3D printing and Additive Manufacturing, has made the process of creating physical prototypes more cost-effective and efficient. By allowing for the direct creation of an object from a 3D CAD model, these methods significantly reduce production time and costs. When utilized effectively, these prototypes have the potential to decrease the duration of the product development process and/or enhance the final product's quality. Creating physical prototypes presents several challenges, including the time and cost required to construct them, the need for multiple revisions, the testing time needed, the limitations on testing, and the discrepancy between the prototype's performance and the final product's performance. As a result, virtual prototypes are often considered a more attractive option, which will be explored in the next section.

3.7 Virtual Prototyping

Virtual Prototyping is a process of developing a digital model of a product that is yet to be created, also referred to as a "product-to-be". The aim is to enable designers, engineers, and end-users to assess various aspects of the product, such as its aesthetic quality, functionality, ergonomics, and usability. Literature documents several instances where virtual prototyping has been utilized for design evaluation [9–12].

Virtual Prototyping utilizes eXtended Reality (XR) technologies to create and evaluate virtual products, offering realistic visualizations and multimodal interactions that encompass vision, haptic, and auditory modalities (Fig. 3.10). XR technologies are discussed in Chap. 4. A cross-disciplinary approach is necessary for the implementation of a virtual prototype, involving technical fields such as Computer Science, Computer Graphics, Computer Vision, Mechanical Engineering, and Electronics, as well as Human-related disciplines such as Cognitive Psychology and Ergonomics, and Industrial Design.

In the past, virtual testing of upcoming products primarily took place within a virtual environment that heavily relied on powerful visualization capabilities. The virtual prototypes essentially comprised of a lifelike representation of the product, which users could engage with. However, nowadays, cutting-edge stereoscopic visualization technologies offer a remarkably realistic and often high-fidelity visual experience of the virtual product model in real-time [13]. Although this approach is well-suited for assessing the aesthetic qualities of a product, such as variations in colors, textures, and materials under different lighting conditions, it may not be effective in evaluating other aspects, particularly those related to the use and overall user experience of the product.

For many products, particularly those with interactive features, physical interaction and manipulation are critical factors in the evaluation process. However, when evaluating virtual components that lack physicality, the assessment of physical interaction is limited and often produces ineffective results. To address this limitation, advanced virtual prototypes now integrate haptic devices, enabling users to physically interact with the virtual model. This feature allows for the assessment of ergonomics

Fig. 3.10 The practice of virtual prototyping involves using eXtended Reality (XR) technologies to evaluate and validate user eXperiences (UX) that have been designed for a product

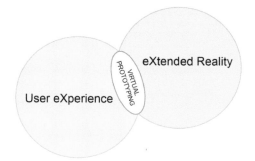

and usability aspects that would otherwise be restricted or impossible with virtual models alone [14].

An alternative approach is the development of mixed prototypes that combine digital and physical elements. This involves incorporating physical objects and components into the virtual environment, which allows for physical interaction. The physical components can be static or dynamic, which can be achieved through the utilization of basic electronic components such as the Arduino board [15].

3.7.1 Benefits of Virtual Prototyping

Virtual prototyping has become a crucial aspect of the product testing phase for several companies across various industries due to its numerous advantages over physical prototyping, which are summarized in Fig. 3.11 and are as follows:

- early evaluation of design elements in the development phase, allowing for earlier decision-making;
- ability to test multiple variants, leading to improved product quality;
- integration of measurement technology to study user performance and impressions;
- lower implementation cost, as only software expenses and time spent coding the prototype are required;
- ability to reuse virtual prototyping components, reducing implementation costs and complexity;
- global sharing of the virtual prototype through digital files and renderings, eliminating the need for physical shipping;
- reduced need for physical prototypes, resulting in time and cost savings.

To sum up, Virtual Prototypes offer more flexibility compared to Physical Prototypes due to their ability to represent a range of design alternatives by varying parameters in the digital model. They are also easier and cheaper to modify. However,

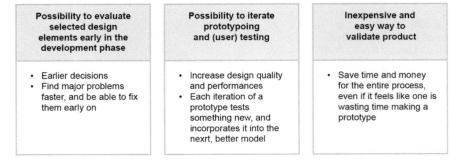

Fig. 3.11 Overview of benefits of virtual prototyping

Physical Prototypes are necessary to detect unanticipated phenomena, which cannot be revealed in Virtual Prototypes. Thus, at least one Physical Prototype is typically built-in product development efforts.

References

1. Harvard Business Review. https://hbr.org/2011/04/why-most-product-launches-fail. Last accessed 15 May 2023
2. Bloch PH (2011) Product design and marketing: reflections after fifteen years. J Prod Innov Manag 28(3):378–380
3. ISO 9241. https://www.iso.com. Last accessed 15 May 2023
4. Designing Our Tomorrow. http://www.designingourtomorrow.com/. Last accessed 15 May 2023
5. Ulrich KT, Eppinger SD (2019) Yang, 7th edn. M.C, Product design and development
6. Hartson R, Pyla P (2018) The UX book—agile UX design for a quality user experience, 2nd edn. Science Direct
7. Bourell DL, Beaman JJ, Wohlers T (2020) History of additive manufacturing. Additive manufacturing processes, vol. 24. In: Bourell DL, Frazier W, Kuhn H, Seifi M (eds) ASM handbook, ASM International, pp 11–18
8. Unity3D. https://unity.com. Last accessed 15 May 2023
9. Horiuchi S, Kanai S, Kishinami T, Hosoda S, Ohshima Y, Shiroma Y (2005) Low-cost and rapid prototyping of UI-embedded mock-ups using RFID and its application to usability testing. In: Proceedings of HCII 2005 conference
10. Aoyama H, Nordgren A, Yamaguchi H, Komatsu Y, Ohno M (2007) Digital style design systems from concept to sophisticated shape. Int J Interact Des Manuf 1:55–65
11. Jayaram S, Vance J, Gadh R, Jayaram U, Srinivasan H (2001) Assessment of VR technology and its applications to engineering problems. J Comput Inf Sci Eng 1(1):72
12. Vo DM, Vance JM, Marasinghe MG (2009) Assessment of haptics-based interaction for assembly tasks in virtual reality. In: Proceedings of world haptics 2009
13. Azuma R, Baillot Y, Behringer R, Feiner S, Julier S, MacIntyre B (2001) Recent advances in augmented reality. IEEE Comput Graphics Appl 21(6):34–47
14. Jones L (2018) Haptics. The MIT Press
15. Arduino Board. https://www.arduino.cc. Last accessed 15 May 2023

Chapter 4
Multisensory Interaction in eXtended Reality

Abstract This chapter provides an overview of eXtended Reality (XR), a term that encompasses technologies such as Virtual Reality (VR), Augmented Reality (AR), and Mixed Reality (MR). XR allows the real world to be enriched with virtual data, objects, and information, offering varying levels of immersion and interaction. The chapter explores the components of XR and discusses classification frameworks, including Milgram's Reality-Virtuality Continuum and the 3I model. It further delves into the developments and technologies of VR, highlighting stereoscopic vision, VR headsets and immersive walls. The chapter also explores AR, its accessibility through everyday devices, and its applications. The importance of considering all sensory modalities for creating immersive XR experiences is emphasized, and the role of multimodal interaction in enhancing user experiences is discussed. The chapter highlights the significance of a multisensory approach in achieving a sense of presence and explores examples of early immersive and multisensory technology. Finally, it discusses the impact of touch in human interaction and the incorporation of tactile sensations in VR applications, as well as of olfaction, which plays a significant role in human perception and memory, as certain smells can evoke strong emotional responses and trigger vivid recollections of past experiences. Incorporating odors into XR applications can enhance the overall sense of presence and realism by providing users with scent cues that align with the virtual environment. Olfactory displays are devices that release specific odors or scents to accompany virtual content.

eXtended Reality, often named XR, is a term that is becoming increasingly popular and refers to a set of technologies that allow the real world to be enriched with virtual data, objects, and information. This term encompasses Virtual Reality and Augmented Reality, as well as any future integrations of the real and virtual domains.

XR encompasses a range of technologies that offer varying levels of fidelity and immersion, from fully virtual experiences to those that augment the real world. These technologies allow us to create interactive content that can be perceived by users as if they were real. The level of immersion is influenced by the level of realism of the interaction, with more realistic interactions leading to a higher level of immersion.

To gain a deeper understanding of eXtended Reality and its potential applications, it is necessary to examine its various components. eXtended Reality (XR) comprises

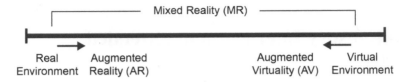

Fig. 4.1   Reality-virtuality continuum [1]

a combination of Virtual Reality (VR), Augmented Reality (AR), and Mixed Reality (MR).

Two frameworks that have been developed to classify and describe these technologies are the Reality-Virtuality Continuum, which was proposed by Milgram et al. [1], and the 3I (Immersion, Interaction, and Imagination) model, introduced by Burdea and Coiffet [2]. Figure 4.1 depicts Milgram's Reality-Virtuality Continuum.

At one end of Milgram's Continuum is *Virtual Reality* (VR), which is likely the most well-known technology in the continuum. VR refers to the use of computer technology to generate a simulated experience that can be either similar to or completely different from the real world. VR experiences typically include visuals and sounds that are presented through VR headsets or multi-projection systems.

The origins of virtual experiences date back to the 1950s, when Morton Heilig wrote about a theater that could provide an all-encompassing sensory experience [3]. Jaron Lanier is widely credited as the father of Virtual Reality, having popularized the term and founded VPL Research in the 1980s, one of the first companies to produce and sell virtual reality products.

Virtual Reality applications rely on VR headsets, also known as Head Mounted Displays (HMDs), as their main technology [4]. These HMDs consist of small screens placed in front of the eyes that provide video feedback. By wearing HMDs, users are completely immersed in the simulated virtual environment and are unable to see the world around them, as the headsets block ambient light.

The development of VR headsets is expected to progress rapidly in the coming years. There are already many companies investing heavily in VR technology and competing to create more advanced and affordable VR headsets. With the increasing demand for immersive virtual experiences, it is expected that the development of VR headsets will continue to improve and become more accessible to the general public.

Current high-end HMDs are self-contained wireless devices that do not rely on a PC or smartphone for delivering the VR experience. They come with built-in processors, GPS, sensors, and batteries. Examples of popular HMDs include the Oculus Quest [5] and the HTC Vive [6].

To enhance the immersive experience in VR, some headsets incorporate additional features such as headphones, motion sensors, and controllers. Headphones are used in VR to provide spatial audio, which enhances the sense of presence in a virtual environment. For example, in a VR game where you are exploring a forest, the sound of birds chirping can be heard coming from the direction they are in, adding to the feeling that you are really there. The motion sensors in the HMD track the user's head movements and adjust the virtual camera in real-time to create a more immersive experience. This allows the user to look around the virtual environment just as they would in the real world. VR controllers are used to track the movement of the user's hands and body, allowing for more realistic interactions in a virtual environment. For example, in a VR game where you are using a sword to battle enemies, the controller can track your movements and make the sword move accordingly in the virtual world.

Stereoscopy is a technique that takes advantage of the way the human visual system works to create an illusion of depth in a moving image. The human brain perceives depth based on the slight differences between the images seen by each eye, which are then combined into a single image with depth perception. Stereoscopy works by displaying two slightly different images, one for each eye, which then creates the illusion of depth. When these two images are viewed through special glasses that filter each image to the corresponding eye, the brain interprets them as a single 3D image with depth [7]. This is how stereoscopic 3D works in VR applications, and it can be particularly effective in creating a more immersive and realistic experience for the viewer.

Instead of using headsets, there are other ways to experience VR environments such as using large screens and stereo eyewear for stereoscopic vision. One effective method, although expensive, is through the use of a VR CAVE. The CAVE was invented by a group of researchers at the University of Illinois in 1992 [8]. A CAVE is a space dedicated to virtual reality that utilizes the walls, floor, and ceiling as projection screens, creating a highly immersive environment. To interact with the virtual objects, users wear stereoscopic eyewear and use input devices such as VR controllers, data gloves, or joysticks. For instance, architects can use a CAVE to virtually walk through and explore their designs, allowing them to identify potential flaws or areas for improvement before the building is actually constructed. This can save time and money in the construction process and lead to a better final product. The immersive environment of a CAVE allows architects to experience the design at a scale and level of detail that would not be possible with traditional 2D plans or even 3D models on a computer screen.

In relation to Milgram's Continuum, *Augmented Reality* (AR) is located adjacent to the Real Environment. AR is a technology that superimposes virtual objects and information onto the real world, enriching the user's experience with digital elements such as images, texts, animations, videos, and audios. Unlike VR, AR does not seek to replace the real world, but rather enhance it.

AR is currently the most popular form of eXtended Reality due to its versatility and accessibility. One reason for its success is that AR applications can be used on everyday devices, such as smartphones and tablets, making it easy and intuitive for users to engage with. By using the device's camera, AR software can capture the real world and superimpose virtual content on top of it. This is especially advantageous as these devices are typically affordable, making AR accessible to a wide range of people. Additionally, AR can be integrated with other technologies such as AR glasses and headsets, allowing users to experience AR environments and content without having to hold a device. Some examples of AR headsets are the Epson Moverio [9] and the Vuzix Blade Smart Glasses and M300 [10].

AR's primary advantage is that users can engage with and perceive the real-world environment around them, without being isolated. However, AR's weakness is that the level of interaction with virtual content is limited, leading to a lower sense of immersion. AR is widely used, including in popular smartphone apps like Snapchat filters [11], as well as cultural [12] and industrial applications for training and maintenance [13]. AR is predicted to have the highest potential for widespread adoption.

Augmented Virtuality (AV), the second intermediary point in the Virtuality Continuum, involves incorporating real-world objects into a virtual environment. AV encompasses virtual spaces that allow for real-time interaction between physical elements, such as people or objects, and the virtual world. A range of techniques can achieve this integration, such as streaming video from physical spaces or utilizing 3-dimensional digitalization of physical objects.

Milgram's Continuum includes all types of technology within the *Mixed Reality* (MR) category. However, in modern usage, MR refers specifically to forms of eXtended Reality that merge the real and virtual environments to create a new environment where virtual and real objects can coexist and interact in real-time. MR offers a high level of interactivity and a moderate level of immersion. This technology, also known as *Hybrid Reality*, demands significant processing power and can be experienced using specialized glasses. For example, Microsoft's HoloLens has a transparent display, integrated sensors, speakers, and its own computing unit, allowing users to overlay virtual objects onto the real world and interact with them [14].

eXtended Reality (XR) is a broad term that encompasses all environments and interactions that merge physical and virtual elements. The previously discussed VR, AR, and MR technologies are all considered part of XR. Interest in these technologies is on the rise, with recent market research showing a growing number of consumers interested in the phenomenon of XR and its applications. According to numerous studies, XR is expected to become a mainstream phenomenon in the coming years.

4.1   Immersion, Interaction and Imagination in VR

Figure 4.2 illustrates the 3I model, introduced by Burdea and Coiffet [2]. Immersion, interaction, and imagination are the three key components of virtual reality that make it such a unique and exciting technology.

In VR environments, the level of immersion and interaction is typically very high.

Immersion refers to the sense of being surrounded by a virtual environment. Immersion is defined as "a psychological state characterized by perceiving oneself to be enveloped by [...] an environment that provides a continuous stream of stimuli and experiences" [15, p. 227], allowing users to feel physically present in a nonphysical world. Many VR applications use images, sounds, and other stimuli to create an engrossing environment and enhance the perception of immersion.

Fig. 4.2 Virtual reality 3I
model by Burdea and Coiffet
[2]

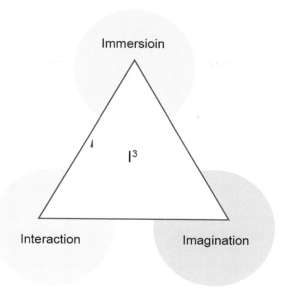

For example, a user wearing a VR headset can feel as if they are inside a game, interacting with the virtual world and experiencing the sights and sounds in a way that feels realistic. Another example is the VR simulation of a deep-sea dive. The user would wear a VR headset and be surrounded by a 360-degree view of the ocean floor, with realistic graphics, lighting, and sound effects. As the user moves through the environment, they would encounter different types of marine life and interact with the environment, feeling as if they were really in the ocean. The VR experience could also incorporate haptic feedback, such as vibrations or pressure changes, to simulate the feeling of being underwater.

Interaction is another key component of virtual reality. Interaction "refers to the degree to which users of a medium can influence the form or content of the mediated environment" [16, p. 80]. In immersive VR environments, users can move around, interact with virtual objects and features, and act and react to events and situations. In a virtual environment, users can also interact with objects and other users in ways that are not possible in the real world. For example, imagine a VR training program for surgeons. The user wears a VR headset and is transported to a virtual operating room, where they can practice performing surgeries on virtual patients. The user has access to virtual surgical tools, such as scalpels, forceps, and sutures, and can use them to perform various procedures. This level of interaction helps to create a sense of presence within the virtual environment and makes the experience more engaging.

Finally, imagination refers to the creative aspect of virtual reality. Virtual environments can be designed to simulate real-world environments, such as a cityscape, a shopfloor, or a natural landscape, or they can be completely imaginary, such as a fantasy land. The only limit to what can be created in a virtual environment is the designer's imagination. This aspect of virtual reality allows users to explore and experience worlds that they would not otherwise have access to.

4.2 Multisensory Interaction

Creating XR applications and experiences is a significant challenge as it requires presenting virtual content to users in a realistic way that closely replicates real-world experiences with a high degree of accuracy. Additionally, seamlessly integrating the real and virtual aspects of the experience is crucial.

By leveraging XR technologies, it is possible to provide users with high-quality experiences where they can interact with objects and environments that closely resemble their daily experiences, rather than feeling like they are engaging with something artificial. This can have a profound impact on users' moods and emotions during the XR experience, ultimately affecting their performance, enjoyment, and the quality of their interactions with the virtual environment and objects.

Achieving convincing XR experiences requires considering how humans perceive information from the external world and how they interact and communicate with it. Humans interact with the world around them through their senses of touch, sight, hearing, taste, and smell, rarely experiencing these senses in isolation. Rather, human physical interaction with the environment is inherently multisensory, integrating information from various independent channels to form a coherent percept of the world [17]. Therefore, to create an immersive virtual experience, all senses must be stimulated in a convincing and coherent manner to replicate the same multisensory experience as in the real world.

Regarding computer-generated environments, multimodal human–computer interaction involves interacting with the virtual and physical environment through natural modes of communication [18]. These systems can offer flexible, efficient, and usable environments, allowing users to interact using input modalities such as speech, hand gestures, and gaze, and receiving information from the system through output modalities such as 3D visualization, speech synthesis and sounds, haptic cues, and smells. This approach allows for more natural and intuitive interactions, enhancing the user experience and increasing the potential for adoption and commercial success.

At present, multimodal output for XR applications primarily consists of visual and auditory cues, with graphics being the main component to achieve a fully immersive experience, since they are considered the most important senses for communicating information. In fact, in our daily lives, a significant amount of information is conveyed through visual means such as images, texts, and videos, and through auditory means such as sounds, speech, and music. Many of the communication tools and objects we use daily are based on these two senses. Moreover, the sense of sight is often considered dominant and has been extensively studied over the years [19]. However, to truly emulate any real-world experience, all senses must be included. While humans are primarily visual creatures, incorporating other sensory cues can expand processing capabilities and lead to faster acquisition and retention of information, as evidenced by findings in cognitive science related to multimodal interaction [20]. Furthermore, studies in neuroscience and psychology demonstrate that human perception is naturally multisensory, relying on the integration of input from multiple sensory modes when engaging with the surrounding environment [21].

Therefore, to achieve a truly immersive XR experience, it is essential to consider all sensory modalities and design appropriate cues for each of them. To create a more immersive and convincing experience, XR applications are beginning to incorporate other senses, such as touch and olfaction, in addition to visual and auditory cues (Fig. 4.3). This is referred to as *multisensory interaction*, where multiple sensory modalities intersect to construct a meaningful representation of the environment and its content. When the different stimuli perceived through the various senses are consistent with each other, the user's perceptual system recognizes virtual objects and environments as real, creating a sense of presence.

Design and development of XR experiences is not simply a matter of adding up individual sensory stimuli, but rather involves a complex interplay between the different senses that can lead to more nuanced and rich perceptions [22]. This underscores the crucial role of a multi-sensory approach in creating immersive XR experiences, which are often evaluated based on the user's "Sense of Presence". This psychological construct is essential for creating a realistic experience in XR environments and can be measured through self-report measures such as questionnaires [23]. By incorporating multiple senses in an XR application, the user's Sense of Presence can be enhanced, resulting in a more engaging and believable experience.

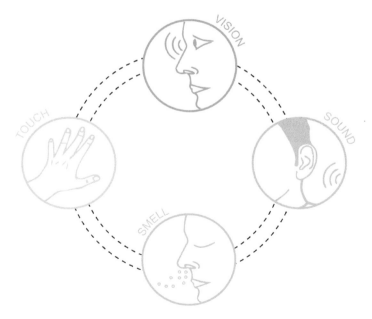

Fig. 4.3 The four senses simulated in multisensory XR applications

The use of the multisensory approach has been a focus in the VR, AR and MR field since their inception, with the development of devices and machines aimed at engaging all human senses. The Sensorama, one of the earliest known examples of immersive and multisensory technology, was the first application to propose this approach. Invented by Morton Heilig in 1961, the Sensorama is a mechanical device that comprises a stereoscopic color display, fans, odor emitters, a stereo sound system, and a motional chair [24]. It creates an experience that simulates a motorcycle ride through New York city by having the spectator sit in an imaginary motorcycle while experiencing the street through the screen, fan-generated wind, and simulated noise and smells of the city.

The importance of using a multisensory approach when designing user experiences is already well-known in the fields of product design, art, and marketing. In the past few years, numerous research and practical initiatives focused on the multisensory approach have been conducted in various sectors, including commercial ones such as the gaming industry, as well as the cultural heritage and industrial sectors. For instance, the implementation of a multisensory approach in the cultural heritage domain has shown significant improvements in the sense of presence and overall perceived immersion, as well as user engagement in virtual environments. This has been reported in [25] and highlights the impact of the multisensory augmented reality application on visitors' sense of presence, enjoyment, knowledge, and value of the experience. The paper showed that the usage of the various stimuli, i.e., combinations of visual, audio and smell stimuli, depend on the goal of the experience. For example, smell should be used to privilege realism and spatial presence, while audio should be adopted when the goal is to elicit involvement.

4.3   The Sense of Touch and Haptic Interaction

Humans perceive objects through touch, which is the third most utilized sense. By touching, pressing, and manipulating objects, humans can interact with them. For example, humans can press buttons or points on a screen or move objects to different positions in space, such as with a mouse. The significance of touch in human interaction is further emphasized by the fact that it is the first sense to develop, even before sight [26].

Touch has a crucial role to play both in emotional and perceptual aspects, even when the user is not consciously aware of its utilization [27]. The sense of touch is significant not only in interpersonal communication but also in interacting with objects. This is primarily because touch, often referred to as "the most stimulating" of human senses, has been demonstrated to impact human emotions [28].

In recent years, advertising techniques have increasingly incorporated tactile sensations to establish stronger emotional and cognitive links between the consumer and the product or brand. Notably, activating this part of the brain has been found to be associated with consumers' willingness to pay a higher price for a product. Additionally, a recent study revealed that the psychophysiological responses generated by materials in contact with our skin are considerably greater than those elicited by sight alone [29]. In other words, contact with objects elicits physiological reactions linked to our behavior and emotions more significantly than their mere visual appearance.

The term "haptics" encompasses technologies that engage users' tactile senses, specifically, the sense of touch experienced upon contact with an object. Haptics refers to the scientific study of touch in both real-world and virtual environments [30]. This involves investigating not only human touch capabilities but also designing engineering systems to create haptic virtual environments. Technically speaking, haptics pertains to touch feedback technology that is utilized when interacting with computer-generated simulations. This technology provides feedback in the form of vibrations, force, and motion.

Haptic technology comprises end effectors, sensors, actuators, computers, real-time algorithms, and application program interfaces. Initially, haptic technology was primarily used in tele-manipulation systems. The first haptic robotic manipulator was deployed at the Argonne National Lab in 1954, and the haptic technology utilized a master–slave tele-manipulation system [31].

Since its inception, haptic technology has undergone significant advancements. The first haptic devices were based on electromagnetic technologies, such as vibratory motors, which predominantly provided feedback through vibrations. In contrast, modern haptic technologies are capable of providing multi-level feedback based on the user's exerted force. Most haptic technologies consist of grounded interfaces like Phantom devices [32] or glove-type haptic displays, such as exoskeletons like the CyberGrasp [33].

Newer wearable haptic devices are designed to be untethered and ungrounded, and they directly interact with the skin [34]. These devices offer greater freedom and a larger workspace than grounded systems and are better suited for human–computer interaction tools used in mobile applications.

Research in the field of haptics has gained momentum in recent years. Various companies focused on VR are actively developing advanced haptic technologies with a range of solutions. For instance, Ultraleap's Mid-Air Haptics [35] supports hand tracking and mid-air haptic feedback, Hi5 VR glove [36] captures full hand and finger movements in VR, HaptX DK2 VR Glove [37] allows users to interact with heavy objects in VR, and Teslasuit for Full-Body Haptics [38] combines haptic feedback, motion capture, and biometrics to deliver a full-body sensory experience in VR.

Current research is exploring future haptic technologies such as handheld haptics that can support large-scale body movement and eliminate the limitations of wearable haptic technology such as weight, complex wiring, and constrained hand movement. In addition, haptic technologies using ultrasound waves are being developed to eliminate the need for physical devices to haptically sense virtual objects. An example is the Ultrahaptics technology, which creates the sense of touch in mid-air [39]. It allows users to touch and feel virtual objects without the need for wearing physical devices.

Anticipated advancements in haptic technology are expected to render physical devices unnecessary for detecting virtual objects. With the cost of haptic devices decreasing rapidly, their availability in the market is increasing, enabling their use in a wide range of applications.

The integration of haptic feedback significantly enhances user experience when interacting with simulated environments, objects, and situations. Haptic technology can play a crucial role in the product development process, particularly in testing design properties, like product ergonomics, and manufacturing aspects, like component assembly and disassembly. By utilizing haptic technology for such activities, it enables a more thorough understanding of the product's functionality, reducing the necessity for multiple physical prototyping iterations.

A study on multisensory application for virtual product testing is presented in [40, 41], which focuses on the virtual testing of a commercial washing machine to evaluate how customers perceive the quality of the product. The manufacturers of such products believe that customers typically judge the quality of a product based on their direct interaction with certain elements, such as the knob, detergent drawer, and door. When faced with two products of similar price and technical specifications, customers often make purchasing decisions based on perceived quality. Therefore, it is advantageous for designers to obtain users' preferences before the end of the design process and incorporate these parameters into the project specification. To achieve this goal, a multisensory virtual prototype of a washing machine has been developed, which includes a 3D stereoscopic representation of its aesthetic appearance, tactile feedback of interactive elements such as the door, drawer, knob, and buttons provided through a 6DOF (Degrees Of Freedom) force-feedback device, and sounds produced by these elements during their use. The components of the washing machine with which the user can interact are depicted in Fig. 4.4 and include the drawer, knob, buttons, and door.

Fig. 4.4 Multisensory virtual prototyping for product quality evaluation [40]

4.4 Olfaction and Olfactory Displays

The sense of smell holds great significance in our daily existence as it performs a vital function in sensing and understanding chemical signals in the surroundings. This sense assists in essential biological and behavioral activities, including the identification of potential dangers, locating food sources, and facilitating social communication [42].

Additionally, due to the involvement of multiple regions of the brain in the process of olfaction, odors can evoke memories and emotional responses even before they are consciously recognized. This makes them valuable in improving a person's mood, enhancing learning and attention, and evoking emotions [43].

The connection between odors and memory is particularly strong, and research has been conducted in various fields such as basic science, marketing, and psychology to understand the effects of odors. Pleasant odors have been shown to induce positive moods, while unpleasant ones can have the opposite effect [44]. Odors can also induce states of activation or relaxation and stimulate cognitive abilities.

Western society has often been referred to as "the society of olfactory silence" [45] due to the historical tendency to eliminate unpleasant odors. However, in recent times, the importance of smell has gained recognition, particularly for its ability to stimulate emotions and enhance product experiences when combined with other sensory modalities. This aspect has been extensively studied in the marketing research field, with a focus on the use of odors to influence customers' moods in stores [46], and to communicate information about products [47].

Furthermore, odors can also serve as a means of communicating information about products, such as perfumes, household cleaners, and food. In the mass market, the quality of products is often perceived through their associated odors [48]. As a result, companies add fragrances to various commercial products, including soaps and household cleaners.

Various studies have investigated the impact of olfaction and olfactory stimuli on the other senses. Dematté et al. conducted research that demonstrated that female participants tend to rate male faces as less attractive when presented with an unpleasant odor compared to a situation where the faces are presented with a pleasant scent or odorless medical air [49]. Similarly, a study revealed the influence of olfactory stimuli on the evaluation of commercial products [50]. This highlights the reason why odors are increasingly being used in marketing campaigns.

Numerous studies have explored the interplay between olfaction and vision. For instance, Moessnang et al. [51] demonstrated that olfactory stimuli can affect visual perception, while Gottfried and Dolan [52] investigated the use of visual cues in odor identification. They conducted testing sessions where participants were asked to identify a smell as quickly as possible while viewing a congruent or incongruent image. Their results showed that the detection of odors was faster and more accurate when the visual counterpart was congruent with the odor. Over the years, numerous studies have aimed to investigate the influence of vision on olfaction and the effects of visual stimuli such as colors and images on olfactory perception [53]. A summary of these studies can be found in recent surveys [54].

To achieve a satisfactory result in a multi-sensory XR experience, it is crucial to incorporate the sense of smell. Olfactory Displays (ODs) are computer-controlled devices that generate scented air and deliver it to the human olfactory organ (as shown in Fig. 4.5). Since humans perceive smells through the air, the OD's role is to create scented air from stocked smell materials, with the desired components and concentration, and to deliver it to the human olfactory organ [55]. Scented air is typically generated through vaporization or atomization processes of stocked smell materials in liquid, oil, or powder form, and delivered through air flow, tubes, or direct injection. Unlike colors, odors cannot be obtained through combinations of primary odors. Therefore, ODs can only deliver a limited number of odors that depend on what is stocked in the device. Additionally, the perception of odors is subjective and can vary from person to person. Therefore, ODs must allow the tuning of the intensity and duration of smell effects.

Olfactory Displays can take the form of wearable devices that are worn by the user or devices placed in the environment. Wearable ODs have the advantage of being able to present minimal amounts of scent stimuli as they are close to the user's olfactory field, but they can be bulky and inconvenient for the user. On the other hand, displays placed in the environment may not be noticed by the user until their olfactory sense is stimulated by the olfactory media component, but the delivery of olfaction can be significantly affected by the user's movements in the environment.

In the past few years, several ODs have become commercially available, some of which are integrated into headsets. For instance, the VAQSO scent device [56] can be attached to various Head Mounted Displays and has the ability to hold up to five replaceable scent cartridges. Another example is the FEELREAL scent generator [57], which is compatible with most HMDs and contains a replaceable cartridge with nine aroma capsules. Additionally, the OLORAMA digital smell simulator [58] can be placed in the environment and integrates up to ten realistic scents.

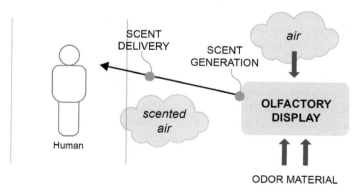

Fig. 4.5 Olfactory displays working principle

a   b

Fig. 4.6 XR application for virtual product evaluation: **a** integrated HMD and OD; **b** virtual scenario

Carulli et al. [59] presented a study on using multisensory application, including the sense of smell, for virtual product testing. The virtual environment includes three virtual models of commercial washing machines arranged in a virtual room, and the study aims to evaluate various characteristics of the virtual products such as pleasantness of the product's shape and components, perceived usability, perceived value, and purchase intentions (Fig. 4.6). The participants experienced the washing machines alone and in combination with pleasant (lavender) and unpleasant (smoke) odors. The experimental test data analysis revealed that the use of scents had a positive impact on the users' experience of the virtual reality environment and the perceived level of presence. Additionally, the study found that the use of congruent and pleasant scents had a positive influence on the users' evaluations of the product's shape, perceived usability, and value.

Olfactory Displays are increasingly being used to incorporate the sense of smell into multisensory XR applications across various domains such as marketing, healthcare, medical rehabilitation, product design, entertainment, and cultural heritage, as they can significantly enhance users' experiences. However, when designing such multisensory experiences, it is important to consider a holistic approach and ensure that scents are designed and integrated seamlessly with other sensory experiences. To achieve this, virtual and physical prototyping are essential enabling technologies that facilitate the development of interactive prototypes for communication, visualization, and testing of these novel experiences.

References

1. Milgram P, Takemura H, Utsumi A, Kishino F (1995) Augmented reality: a class of displays on the reality-virtuality continuum. In: Proceedings of SPIE 2351, telemanipulator and telepresence technologies
2. Burdea G, Coiffet P (2003) Virtual reality technology, 2nd edn. Wiley-Interscience
3. Moton Heilig. http://www.mortonheilig.com. Last accessed 15 May 2023
4. Sutherland IE (1968) A head-mounted three dimensional display. In: AFIPS '68 (Fall, part I)
5. Oculus. https://www.oculus.com. Last accessed 15 May 2023

6. HTC Vive. https://www.vive.com. Last accessed 15 May 2023
7. Banks MS, Read JC, Allison RS, Watt SJ (2012) Stereoscopy and the human visual system. SMPTE Motion Imaging J 121(4):24–43
8. Cruz-Neira C, Sandin DJ, DeFanti TA, Kenyon RV, Hart JC (1992) The CAVE: audio visual experience automatic virtual environment. Commun ACM 35(6):64–72
9. Epson Moverio. https://moverio.epson.com. Last accessed 15 May 2023
10. Vuzix. https://www.vuzix.com. Last accessed 15 May 2023
11. Snapchat. https://www.snapchat.com. Last accessed 15 May 2023
12. Carulli M, Bordegoni M (2019) Multisensory augmented reality experiences for cultural heritage exhibitions. In: Rizzi C, Andrisano A, Leali F, Gherardini F, Pini F, Vergnano A (eds) Design tools and methods in industrial engineering. Lecture notes in mechanical engineering. Springer
13. Masoni R, Ferrise F, Bordegoni M, Gattullo M, Uva AE, Fiorentino M (2017) Supporting remote maintenance in industry 4.0 through augmented reality. Proc Manuf 11:1296–1302
14. Microsoft Hololens. https://www.microsoft.com/en-us/hololens. Last accessed 15 May 2023
15. Witmer BG, Singer MJ (1998) Measuring presence in virtual environments: a presence questionnaire. Presence Teleoperators Virtual Environ 7(3):225–240
16. Steuer J (1992) Defining virtual reality: dimensions determining telepresence. J Commun 42(4):73–93
17. Burnett S (2011) Perceptual worlds and sensory ecology. Nat Educ Knowl 3(10):75
18. Bourguet ML (2003) Designing and prototyping multimodal commands. In: Proceedings of human-computer interaction (INTERACT'03), pp 717–720
19. Marr D (1982) Vision: a computational investigation into the human representation and processing of visual information. Henry Holt and Co Inc., New York, NY
20. Shams L, Seitz AR (2008) Benefits of multisensory learning. Trends Cogn Sci 12(11):411–417
21. Spence C, Driver J (2004) Crossmodal space and crossmodal attention. Oxford University Press
22. Bordegoni M, Ferrise F (2013) Designing interaction with consumer products in a multisensory virtual reality environment. Virtual Phys Prototyping 8(1):51–64
23. Witmer BG, Singer MJ (1998) Measuring presence in virtual environments: a presence questionnaire. Presence 7(3):225–240
24. Heilig ML (1962) Sensorama simulator, US PAT. 3,050,870
25. Marto A, Melo M, Gonçalves A, Bessa M (2020) Multisensory augmented reality in cultural heritage: impact of different stimuli on presence, enjoyment, knowledge and value of the experience. IEEE Access 8:193744–193756
26. Field TM (1995) Touch in early development. Lawrence Erlbaum Associates, Inc.
27. Gallace A, Spence C (2013) In touch with the future. Oxford University Press
28. Rolls ET, O'Doherty J, Kringelbach ML, Francis S, Bowtell R, McGlone F (2003) Representations of pleasant and painful touch in the human orbitofrontal and cingulate cortices. Cereb Cortex 13(3):308–317
29. Etzi R, Gallace A (2016) The arousing power of everyday materials: an analysis of the physiological and behavioral responses to visually and tactually presented textures. Exp Brain Res 234(6):1659–1666
30. Robles-De-La-Torre G (2006) The importance of the sense of touch in virtual and real environments. IEEE Multim 13(3), Special issue on Haptic User Interfaces for Multimedia Systems, 24–30
31. Argonne National Lab. https://www.anl.gov. Last accessed 15 May 2023
32. Phantom device. https://www.3dsystems.com/haptics-devices/3d-systems-phantom-premium. Last accessed 15 May 2023
33. CyberGrasp. http://www.cyberglovesystems.com/cybergrasp. Last accessed 15 May 2023
34. Pacchierotti C, Sinclair S, Solazzi M, Frisoli A, Hayward V et al (2017) Wearable haptic systems for the fingertip and the hand: taxonomy, review, and perspectives. IEEE Trans Haptics (ToH) 10(4):580–600
35. Ultraleap. https://www.ultraleap.com/haptics/. Last accessed 15 May 2023

36. Ni5vrglove. https://hi5vrglove.com. Last accessed 15 May 2023
37. HaprX. https://haptx.com. Last accessed 15 May 2023
38. Teslasuit. https://teslasuit.io. Last accessed 15 May 2023
39. Ultrahaptics. https://www.ultraleap.com/haptics/. Last accessed 15 May 2023
40. Ferrise F, Bordegoni M, Lizaranzu J (2010) Product design review application based on a vision-sound-haptic interface, haptic and audio interaction design conference. Lecture notes in computer science (LNCS), vol 6306/2010. Springer, pp 169–178
41. Ferrise F, Bordegoni M, Lizaranzu J (2011) Use of interactive virtual prototypes to define product design specifications: a pilot study on consumer product. In: Proceedings of IEEE-ISVRI, Singapore
42. Nakamoto T (2013) Human olfactory displays and interfaces: odor sensing and presentation. Inf Sci Ref
43. Porcherot C, Delplanque S, Raviot-Derrien S, Le Calvé B, Chrea C, Gaudreau N, Cayeux I (2010) How do you feel when you smell this? Optimization of a verbal measurement of odor-elicited emotions. Food Qual Prefer 21:938–947
44. Rétiveau AN, Chambers E IV, Milliken GA (2004) Common and specific effects of fine fragrances on the mood of women. J Sens Stud 19:373–394
45. Corbin A (1986) The foul and the fragrant: Odour and the French social imagination. Harvard University Press
46. Spangenberg ER, Crowley AE (1996) Improving the store environment: do olfactory cues affect evaluations and behaviors? J Mark 60(2):67–80
47. Bosmans A (2006) Scents and sensibility: when do (in)congruent ambient scents influence product evaluations? J Mark 70(3):32–43
48. Gatti E, Bordegoni M, Spence C (2014) Investigating the influence of colour, weight, and fragrance intensity on the perception of liquid bath soap: an experimental study. Food Qual Prefer 31:56–64
49. Demattè ML, Osterbauer R, Spence C (2007) Olfactory cues modulate facial attractiveness. Chem Senses 32(6):603–610
50. Bradford KD, Desrochers DM (2009) The use of scents to influence consumers: the sense of using scents to make cents. J Bus Ethics 90:141–153
51. Moessnang C, Finkelmeyer A, Vossen A, Schneider F, Habel U (2011) Assessing implicit odor localization in humans using a cross-modal spatial Cueing paradigm. PLoS One 6(12)
52. Gottfried JA, Dolan RJ (2003) The nose smells what the eye sees: Crossmodal visual facilitation of human olfactory perception. Neuron 39(2):375–386
53. Zhou W, Zhang X, Chen J, Wang L, Chen D (2012) Nostril-specific olfactory modulation of visual perception in binocular rivalry. J Neurosci 32(48):17225–17229
54. Blackwell L (1995) Visual cues and their effects on odour assessment. Nutr Food Sci 95(5):24–28
55. Yanagida Y, Tomono A (2012) Basics for olfactory display, in human olfactory displays and interfaces. In: Nakamoto T (ed) Odor sensing and presentation. IGI Global
56. Vaqso. https://vaqso.com. Last accessed 15 May 2023
57. Feelreal. https://feelreal.com/. Last accessed 15 May 2023
58. Olorama. https://www.olorama.com/en/. Last accessed 15 May 2023
59. Carulli M, Bordegoni M, Cugini U (2015) Integrating scents simulation in virtual reality multisensory environment for industrial products evaluation. Comput Aided Design Appl

Chapter 5
Case Studies

Abstract This chapter presents selected case studies showcasing the design and testing of user experiences through prototypes created with eXtended Reality (XR) technologies. These case studies were developed by students participating in the Virtual and Physical Prototyping course at the School of Design, Politecnico di Milano. The projects assigned to student teams aimed to create prototypes prioritizing user interaction and experience, such as apps connecting young people with nature or aiding language learning. The students followed a simplified product development process, starting with defining the target audience and requirements, followed by concept development and design execution, and appropriate XR technologies selection for the implementation. The chapter presents a set of guidelines that outline this simplified product development process for crafting XR application prototypes. Subsequent chapters showcase how these guidelines were applied by the students in their respective case studies.

This chapter showcases some selected case studies that illustrate the design and testing of user experiences through prototypes created with eXtended Reality (XR) technologies. These case studies were produced by the students participating in the Virtual and Physical Prototyping (VPP) course taught by the authors at the School of Design, Politecnico di Milano.

The students have been grouped into 2–4 member teams. Each team has been assigned a project for the final exam. The projects were introduced to the students with an objective and brief overview, along with specific requirements. The objectives of most of the projects revolve around creating prototypes of products and applications that prioritize user interaction and user experience. Some examples of objectives include "designing an app that connects young people with nature for stress relief", or "developing an app that aids users in learning foreign languages".

As outlined in Chap. 3 of this book, the typology and properties of prototyping dictate that the prototypes developed by the students serve the purpose of presenting their ideas about the product or application to the professors and classmates, and to validate the concept by assessing its compliance with the requirements. The students were asked to create prototypes that are as comprehensive as possible in relation to the objective and of a high-fidelity nature.

The students conceptualized and designed the application using the guidelines outlined in the subsequent section, which also included the choice of the most appropriate XR technology from those available in the University labs. The XR applications were created using Unity, Unity Mars, and Vuforia—software platforms covered in the course.

Unity is a game development platform created by Unity technology and released in 2005 [1]. It is widely utilized by developers to create high-quality 2D and 3D games, interactive simulations, and other immersive experiences and to distribute them across various platforms including mobile devices, desktops, VR/AR devices, consoles, and the web, while also integrating with visualization and interaction technologies. Currently, the platform is employed in a range of industries beyond video gaming, including architecture, engineering, film, automotive, construction, medicine, and others.

Unity MARS, an acronym for Mixed and Augmented Reality Studio, is an extension of the Unity platform that provides functionality for creating Augmented (AR) and Mixed Reality (MR) content [2].

Vuforia is an AR and MR development platform from PTC Inc., allowing for the integration of hardware devices, such as mobile devices and MR Head Mounted Displays (HMD) [3].

Unity MARS and Vuforia enable the development of eXtended Reality applications, and both include an important tracking function, which enables the recognition and tracking of specific images to overlay digital content accurately. In AR and MR applications, markers are images or objects registered with the application that serve as information triggers. Both Unity MARS and Vuforia primarily utilize marker-based tracking but also employ plane-tracking, face-tracking, and other tracking methods. When the device's camera recognizes these markers in the real world, the AR/MR application activates the display of virtual content in the camera view, aligned with the marker's position in the physical world.

Marker-based tracking can utilize a range of marker types, including QR codes, image targets, and 2D tags. The simplest and most prevalent marker used in AR/MR applications is an Image Target, which is an image registered manually by the developer with the XR application and serves as a trigger for displaying virtual content. Usually, image targets are images with clear shapes and complicated outlines, making them easy for the image recognition and tracking algorithms built into the platform to recognize. Examples of image targets can be seen in Fig. 5.1.

Some of the student-created applications link the real and virtual environments through sensors and actuators managed by Arduino boards [4]. Arduino is an open-source electronics platform that is user-friendly and accessible to anyone, even those without advanced programming skills, making it ideal for creating interactive projects. With Arduino, it is possible to quickly and easily create small devices such as light controllers, motor speed controllers, light sensors, temperature and humidity control automation, and many other projects that utilize sensors, actuators, and communication.

The students used a variety of software to develop their XR content. The majority of them utilized Adobe Suite and Figma [5] for creating the GUI structure and 2D

Fig. 5.1 Examples of image targets used in XR applications

elements, and 3D modeling software like SolidWorks, Rhinoceros, and Blender for the creation of 3D models.

Additionally, some of the students utilized assets found on the Unity Assets Store [6] in their projects to enhance their 3D models and 2D elements, as well as to simplify the design of complex interactions. These assets often include ready-to-use scripts that make it easier to create interactive experiences in VR and AR. Some commonly used assets for basic interactions include Lean Touch, Lean GUI, and Lean Localization [7].

The integration of these materials has been done to accelerate and simplify the development process for the students, who are at an introductory level. Additionally, using the same materials makes the project more easily replicable.

The following sections highlight some of the projects created by the students to showcase the application of the guidelines and the outcomes achieved. The projects have been organized into three main categories:

- Augmented Reality-powered applications that enhance learning and promote environmental sustainability,
- applications of multisensory experiences in eXtended Reality,
- applications that connect Reality and Virtuality.

5.1 Prototyping Guidelines

Before starting the XR application prototype development, the students were given guidelines to follow a simplified version of the product development process, considering the time constraints and limited resources. The workflow is depicted in Fig. 5.2.

The first step in the process was to determine the target audience and define the requirements and intended use of the application (1). Then, the students developed the concept, i.e., the idea and vision of the application and the design, i.e., how that idea is executed visually and interactively (2).

Fig. 5.2 Workflow for the
development of the
prototypes of the XR
applications

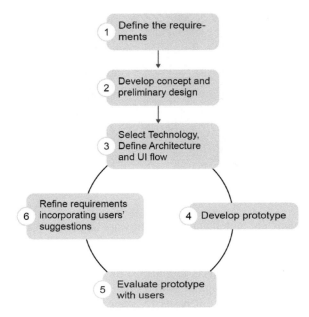

The concept defines the overall idea or vision of what the application is meant to do and the problem it is intended to solve. It includes identifying the target audience, defining the application's features and functions, and determining the goals and objectives of the application. The students presented multiple concepts that were reviewed and discussed with the professors to select the best idea and ensure it met the requirements.

The design consists of the visual and interactive elements that make up the User Interface (UI) and User eXperience (UX) of the application. It involves creating sketches, wireframes, mockups of the application's (for instance, screens, layout, navigation, shape, functions, etc.) to ensure that the final product looks and feels appealing, intuitive, and easy to use.

Afterward, the students selected the most appropriate eXtended Reality technology from those taught in class to implement their project, and established the application architecture, which involved organizing and integrating various components and modules (3). When necessary, they were also required to outline the user interaction flow using tools such as flow charts, state diagrams, or mind maps.

The implementation of the XR application was carried out using Unity, Unity MARS, or Vuforia, with the possibility of connecting with sensors and actuators (4). The goal of prototyping is to create simple products and applications with minimal effort, and incorporating pre-existing models and materials aligns with this objective. Therefore, to ensure a quick and efficient development process, the students were given access to basic 3D models of objects and environments, assets, and pre-written code. Additionally, Unity provides developers with access to a variety of 3D models available for download from the Unity Asset Store [6] either for free or at a cost. This approach was taken to speed up the development phase and make it easier for the students, who were at an entry-level, to work with the technology.

Finally, some groups of students conducted testing and evaluation of the prototypes they developed with a group of classmates and friends (5). The System Usability Scale (SUS) questionnaire, a tool used to gauge usability, was utilized during the evaluation phase [8]. It consists of ten questions with five response options ranging from "strongly agree" to "strongly disagree" (as shown in Fig. 5.3).

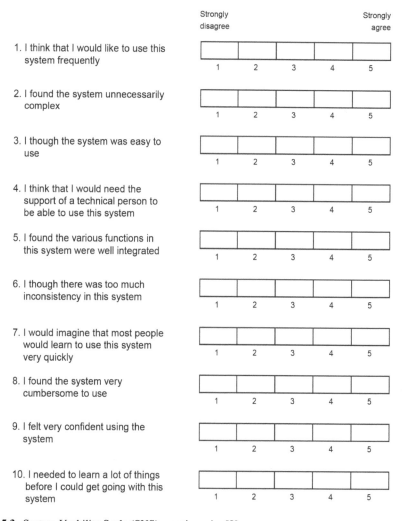

Fig. 5.3 System Usability Scale (SUS) questionnaire [8]

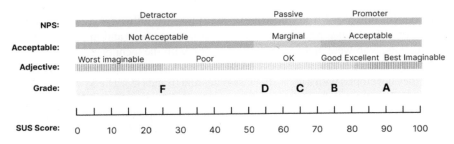

Fig. 5.4 Schema for assessing SUS results [9]

The SUS output can be categorized using Sauro's classification system [9], as shown in Fig. 5.4. This system takes various approaches to interpret the SUS results, including percentiles, grades, adjectives, acceptability, and Net Promoter Score (NPS) customer categories. Additionally, some students performed tests to assess the feeling of presence within the virtual environment. For this purpose, the Presence Questionnaire [10], a ten-item questionnaire adapted from Witmer and Singer's presence questionnaire [11], was primarily utilized. The questions mainly focus on spatial aspects of presence, with responses ranging from 0 to 10 (refer to Fig. 5.5).

The students utilized the test outcomes to modify the specifications of their projects by incorporating user feedback, leading to the refinement of their designs.

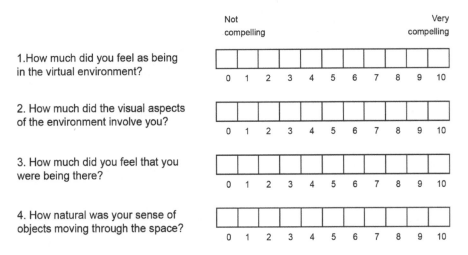

Fig. 5.5 The sense of presence questionnaire [10]

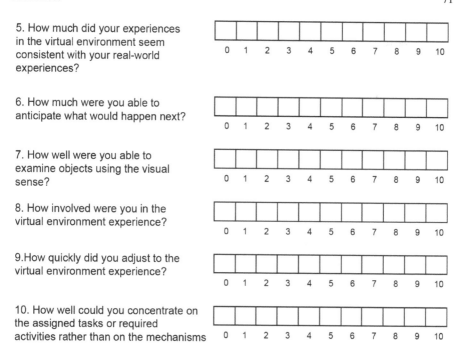

5. How much did your experiences in the virtual environment seem consistent with your real-world experiences?

0 1 2 3 4 5 6 7 8 9 10

6. How much were you able to anticipate what would happen next?

0 1 2 3 4 5 6 7 8 9 10

7. How well were you able to examine objects using the visual sense?

0 1 2 3 4 5 6 7 8 9 10

8. How involved were you in the virtual environment experience?

0 1 2 3 4 5 6 7 8 9 10

9. How quickly did you adjust to the virtual environment experience?

0 1 2 3 4 5 6 7 8 9 10

10. How well could you concentrate on the assigned tasks or required activities rather than on the mechanisms

0 1 2 3 4 5 6 7 8 9 10

Fig. 5.5 (continued)

References

1. Unity. https://unity.com. Last accessed 15 May 2023
2. Unity-MARS. https://unity.com/products/unity-mars. Last accessed 15 May 2023
3. Vuforia. https://www.ptc.com/it/products/vuforia. Last accessed 15 May 2023
4. Arduino Board. https://www.arduino.cc. Last accessed 15 May 2023
5. Figma. https://www.figma.com. Last accessed 15 May 2023
6. Unity Asset Store. https://assetstore.unity.com/. Last accessed 15 May 2023
7. Lean Localization. https://carloswilkes.com/. Last accessed 15 May 2023
8. System Usability Scale (SUS). https://www.usability.gov/how-to-and-tools/methods/system-usability-scale.html. Last accessed 15 May 2023
9. Sauro J. 5 ways to interpret a SUS score. https://measuringu.com/interpret-sus-score/. Last accessed 15 May 2023
10. Lee S, Kim GJ, Lee J (2004) Observing effects of attention on presence with fMRI. In: Proceedings of the ACM symposium on virtual reality software and technology, pp 73–80
11. Witmer BG, Singer MJ (1998) Measuring presence in virtual environments: m presence questionnaire. Presence: Teleoper Virtual Environ 7(3):225–240, 6

Chapter 6
Augmented Reality Applications that Aid in Promoting Sustainability

Abstract In this chapter, three examples are given of how Augmented Reality (AR) technologies can be used to promote sustainability. The initial case study involves an application that illustrates how the environment affects biochemical processes. The second case study features sustainable handmade toys that educate children on electronic circuits. The third one supports children in understanding the entire lifespan of a plant and learning its scientific microscopic processes.

6.1 An AR-Based Application for Teaching the Impact of the Environment on Biochemical Processes

Objective: Design an application that allows teenagers to understand and learn chemical and biological processes by using real-world scenarios.

Description: The activity concerns the design and development of an Augmented Reality application with didactic purposes. By visualizing and interacting with microscopic elements first hand, teenagers can learn about complex biological and chemical cycles and the relationship between natural processes explained and familiar real-world environments. Creating a connection with teenagers' daily lives can help show them effectively how the environment can affect the biochemical cycles and make the sustainability message contained more impactful and memorable.

Requirements: Exploit Augmented Reality technology to create an educational application that can raise curiosity and support teenagers in learning complex chemical and biological topics.

Concept: Target users of the AR educational application consists of students aged 12/13. The application designed aims at supporting teenagers in learning chemistry and biology through visualization and interaction with selected biochemical cycles, i.e., water, carbon, and nitrogen cycles. Real-world scenarios are used to more effectively describe the phenomena since they are familiar to teenagers and can better arouse their interest in both chemistry and biology by showing that these processes exist not only in laboratories but also in the real world. Two real-world scenarios have been selected: natural environment and urban environment.

The application also aims at improving teenagers' awareness of changes caused by natural and artificial substances present in different environmental conditions. They can visualize chemical molecules and elements, and the associated biochemical cycles, that are affected by the different environments in which these cycles occur.

Design: The AR application is designed to be experienced using mobile devices, as tablets and mobile phones.

Figure 6.1 shows the structure of the application. The homepage offers teenagers the possibility to select one of the two environments presented: natural or urban environment.

Two physical posters are created, one representing a natural environment and the second one an urban environment, used as markers for activating AR content, as shown in Fig. 6.2.

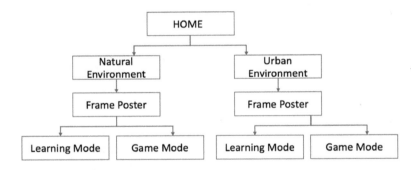

Fig. 6.1 Structure of the application

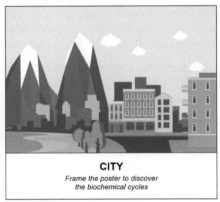

Fig. 6.2 Posters of the natural and urban environments

After selecting one of the two environments via the application, teenagers can frame the corresponding poster to visualize the AR content superimposed on it.

Both environments have two interaction modes that the user can select through the application to learn the specific biochemical cycles and to test the acquired knowledge: the Learning mode and the Game mode. The first mode aims at illustrating the molecules and the biochemical cycles occurring in both environments, while the Game mode aims to check if the concepts explained have been learned correctly.

The Graphical User Interface (GUI) of the application and the posters have been designed using the same playful style. Vivid colors and rounded shapes have been used for the buttons and the cards, recalling the illustration graphics of the posters (Fig. 6.3).

Technology: The application has been developed using Unity 3D [1]. The Augmented Reality component is integrated using Unity MARS [2], and can be used through mobile phones or tablets.

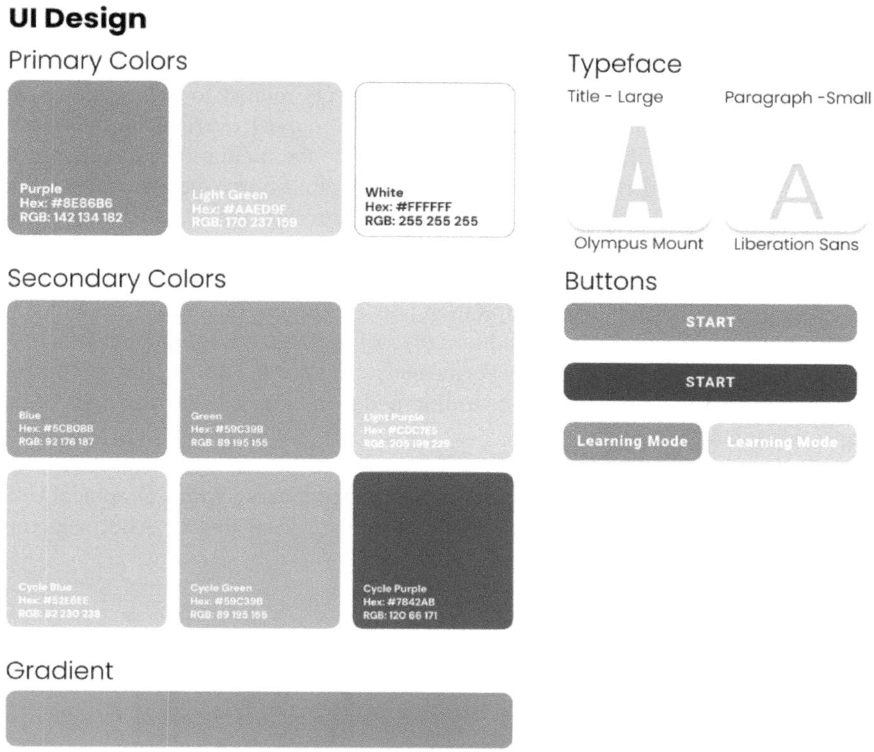

Fig. 6.3 Several components embodying the Graphical User Interface (GUI)

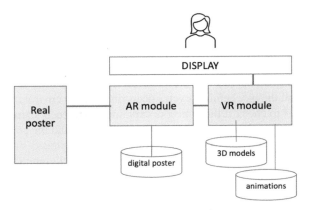

Fig. 6.4 Application architecture

Architecture: The application architecture is made of an Augmented Reality module that displays content on top of the physical posters, and a Virtual Reality module that generates and handles virtual objects and animations (Fig. 6.4).

In the Learning mode, digital 3D and 2D objects related to the environment, such as mountains, water lakes, clouds, and so on, appear overlaid on the poster. The user can click on the virtual objects to visualize the main molecules related to those objects. Then, if interested, they can click again on the specific molecule to view the biochemical cycles of water, carbon, or nitrogen related to it. Each phase of the selected cycle is displayed through animations, showing the effects of the molecular combinations. For example, in the water cycle, the rain and snow effects are integrated to represent the precipitation phases, and the steam effect is added to represent the evaporation phase. Additionally, some effect-related soundtracks have been included to enhance learning performance. Figure 6.5 shows the interaction flow of the application used in the Learning mode, and Fig. 6.6 shows a draft of the graphical layout.

In the Game mode, children are invited to complete the previously learned cycles. After scanning the poster, the 3D and 2D objects appear along with a Graphical User Interface (GUI) menu asking users which cycle they want to test. After selecting

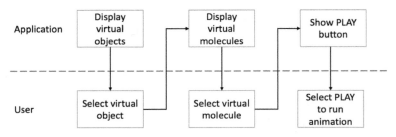

Fig. 6.5 Interaction flow for the learning mode

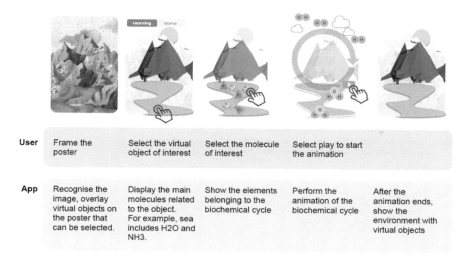

User	Frame the poster	Select the virtual object of interest	Select the molecule of interest	Select play to start the animation	
App	Recognise the image, overlay virtual objects on the poster that can be selected.	Display the main molecules related to the object. For example, sea includes H2O and NH3.	Show the elements belonging to the biochemical cycle	Perform the animation of the biochemical cycle	After the animation ends, show the environment with virtual objects

Fig. 6.6 User inputs and application outputs in learning mode

one of the three cycles, a GUI scheme appears showing the phases of the cycle and the molecules. The scheme contains some blanks that users are asked to fill in to complete the cycle. The teens fill in the blanks by selecting the correct missing molecules from the environment and dragging them into the blanks of the cycle. If the cycle is completed successfully, teens can see an animation of the cycle. Otherwise, error feedback occurs, and they are prompted to rerun the interaction. The error feedback provided considers both the visual and auditory stimulation.

Figure 6.7 shows the interaction flow of the application used in the Game mode, and Fig. 6.8 shows in a draft of the graphical layout.

Implementation: Initially, the students created physical posters, which serve as markers within Unity MARS [2]. Subsequently, they proceeded to design the 3D models associated with the two environments, along with the corresponding animations.

In order to optimize the implementation effort, 3D models of the natural and of the urban environment have been downloaded from the Unity Asset Store [3].

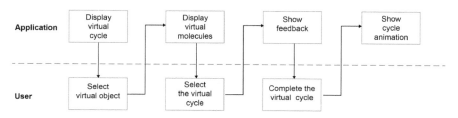

Fig. 6.7 Interaction flow for the game mode

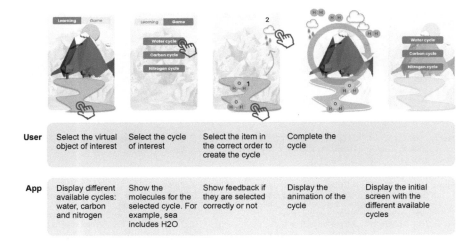

User	Select the virtual object of interest	Select the cycle of interest	Select the item in the correct order to create the cycle	Complete the cycle	
App	Display different available cycles: water, carbon and nitrogen	Show the molecules for the selected cycle. For example, sea includes H2O	Show feedback if they are selected correctly or not	Display the animation of the cycle	Display the initial screen with the different available cycles

Fig. 6.8 User inputs and application outputs in game mode

Instead, the 3D models of the molecules have been created by using Rhinoceros [4]. Then, the markers and the 3D models have been imported into the Unity 3D project, which has been structured into five main scenes, each one corresponding to one of the five application components. The Homepage consists of a GUI that users can use to select and load the other four scenes. The GUI is also used in the other four scenes to allow users to start the cycle view and return to the Homepage. The cycles are represented by using different animations created directly inside Unity. The animations are controlled by using the Animator Controller in Unity, a functionality employed to incorporate animation effects for 3D models. Figure 6.9 depicts a screenshot showcasing the Learning mode of the urban environment.

Credits: Students: Su Uyanik, Selen Saritas, Yerkexhan Nurtazina, Virtual and Physical Prototyping course, School of Design, Politecnico di Milano, Academic Year 20/21.

Video YouTube: https://youtu.be/ZuNYo1w2PDA

6.2 A Tool for AR-Based Learning that Employs Eco-friendly, Handmade Toys for Educating About Circuits

Objective: Creating an Augmented Reality application aimed at educating children on electronic circuits and their components through the use of sustainable, handmade toys.

Fig. 6.9   Screen representing the urban environment Learning mode

Description: Numerous research studies have explored the potential of AR technology as a tool for helping children understand complex scientific and technological subjects, thus making them more accessible [5]. When it comes to scientific experiments and topics, AR offers an opportunity to develop more eco-friendly options in comparison to physical simulations [6]. By leveraging AR, it becomes feasible to produce lifelike effects without the need for physical materials or components, resulting in a zero-waste outcome. According to research [7], only 20% of electronic waste is properly documented, while the fate of approximately 74% is uncertain. It is suspected that a significant portion of this waste is either deposited in landfills, traded, or recycled improperly. Teaching individuals how to recycle electronic circuits could play a vital role in decreasing the volume of waste generated and minimizing the environmental impact of e-waste production. By promoting the recycling of existing components and reducing the need for new electronic devices, we can effectively mitigate the problem.

Requirements: Create a software application that utilizes AR technology to motivate children to participate in both physical and digital activities. The aim is to provide children with accessible and cost-effective learning opportunities, while also incorporating storytelling elements to enhance their enjoyment and engagement. Additionally, the application should include the design of toys made from recycled materials.

Concept: *Toycircuits* is an educational application that utilizes AR technology to teach children (ages 4–6) about electrical circuits and their components through hand-made sustainable toys. The ultimate goal of the experience proposed by the application is to learn about circuits and adopt sustainable behaviors. The application incorporates storytelling to create an interactive and engaging learning experience.

Additionally, *Toycircuits* promotes sustainability by demonstrating how old electronic toy components, such as plugs, electric cords, and batteries, can be recycled to create new toys and reduce e-waste. To enhance the learning experience and captivate children's attention, the application features numerous illustrations and sounds.

The application provides children with the option to choose from four distinct items, each with its own unique story. As the story unfolds, the child is prompted to engage with the AR elements to repair the damaged objects or establish new circuits. Gradually, the interactions become more challenging, introduced one after the other throughout the narrative. Based on input from a kindergarten teacher, as depicted in Table 6.1, the content, styles, sounds, and interactions of the application were defined.

Design: The AR application is designed to be used on mobile devices, and children can use it with the aid of an adult, like a parent or teacher. As for the educational content, the app offers children the chance to gain understanding about different types of components and circuits, spanning from fundamental circuits to more advanced series and parallel circuits. Prior to commencing the AR experience, the first step

Table 6.1 Information gathered through an interview conducted with a teacher from a kindergarten

Question	Answer
What captures children's attention?	Children are intrigued by novelty, enchantment, and the extraordinary. Vibrant colors capture their attention. Children particularly enjoy themes related to nature, fantasy worlds, superheroes, and fairies
Which senses do children rely on the most?	Their primary reliance is on visual and tactile senses
What are the primary subjects that children learn, and what is the duration of each subject?	The class is structured around different activities rather than traditional subjects, such as outdoor games, scientific experiences, and storytelling sessions. Each activity lasts approximately 20 min, but the duration is flexible based on the children's interests
Do children typically engage in individual play or group play?	They usually work in mixed groups of 5 or 6 individuals, with boys and girls often playing their favorite games in separate groups
What types of games are children generally fond of or not fond of?	Children are fond of dramatization, games involving dough, blocks, and graphic-plastic techniques. However, they generally show less interest in directed and overly static games
Are there any specific actions that children find particularly challenging to perform?	At times, fine motor skills can present challenges, and maintaining focus for extended periods (over 20 min) on the same activity can be difficult
Do children show a preference for visual or auditory content?	Children find enjoyment in children's films, animated characters, and themes centered around adventure. Additionally, they have a fondness for music paired with choreographed movements or body actions
Are children already able to read and count?	No, activities mainly revolve around literacy and math preparatory exercises

Mandatory markers: **Optional markers:**

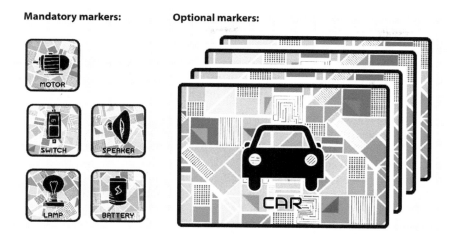

Fig. 6.10 Mandatory and optional AR markers

involves printing the AR markers. The app allows for the direct viewing and downloading of the mandatory and optional markers that children can employ to activate the AR content throughout the experience.

These markers, as depicted in Fig. 6.10, consist of five compact cards that depict electrical components, including a motor, switch, speaker, lamp, and battery, along with four larger cards portraying four different objects: Christmas lights, a robot, a car, and an airplane. The larger cards can be printed optionally in case the child does not possess any old toys or items to recycle and utilize during the experience, providing a foundation for interaction.

After the markers have been printed, the child can begin using the application. Upon visiting the application homepage, they will have the option to select from four different objects to begin the experience: Christmas lights, a robot, a car, and an airplane. Once the child has chosen their desired object, they will be presented with a cartoon-style video that tells a story related to the object and introduces challenges that the child must solve by constructing a circuit. For instance, if the child selects the car object, the video will depict an animated car with issues in its lighting system and ask the child to follow the instructions to fix it. Following this, a guided interaction will be offered: the child will need to scan the pre-printed markers to reveal the electronic components necessary to build the circuit.

Each component of the circuit is depicted in three dimensions and accompanied by educational information presented in both text and audio formats. After the child has identified and selected the appropriate components needed for the circuit, they must place them alternatively on the corresponding large card or old toy. Next, the child must connect all the electronic components correctly to create the circuit by drawing connecting lines using their finger on the device screen. Finally, a positive feedback video displays that the circuit has been successfully repaired and the previously presented problem has been resolved. At this point, the child can return to the homepage and choose another object to continue the experience.

During the application's design process, Gelman's guidelines [8] for designing for children were considered. Specifically, for the target audience of 4–6-year-olds the following guidelines were incorporated into the design:

- integrating learning into the gameplay by presenting educational content when the child scans markers and creates circuits through interaction;
- providing feedback and reinforcement by guiding the interaction with constant instructions and feedback;
- allowing for free-form exploration by letting the child position markers on old objects or the big card and draw connecting lines between components as they see fit;
- keeping the interaction challenging by presenting issues to solve in the form of stories to the child.

Figure 6.11 illustrates an example scenario of the AR application.

Technology: The development of the application involved the use of Unity 3D for virtual content management and Vuforia SDK for Augmented Reality content creation. The graphics and illustrations in the application were created using Figma and Adobe Illustrator, while the 3D models were designed using Rhinoceros [4]. A mobile device is used for running the AR application.

Architecture: The interaction between the user and the system has been managed using the man–machine model proposed by Poelman [9], which is illustrated in Fig. 6.12. The application utilizes various modes of input, including visual cues through the user interface, AR content, and soundtracks. These cues are processed by the user's senses in order to effectively interact with the physical objects and the application. The primary means of user interaction are interface buttons, particularly in the initial stages of the experience, and three-dimensional AR elements that are integrated throughout the experience with the circuits and components.

Implementation: The physical markers necessary for the user to scan during the experience were created at the start of the implementation phase using Adobe Illustrator. Rhinoceros [4] was used to design the 3D models of the circuit components and toys for display in AR, while Adobe Illustrator was used to create the illustrations. Interface elements like buttons, cards, and icons were designed in Figma [10] and exported as individual images for use in Unity. A consistent style was adopted for both the interface elements and markers, with matching colors, fonts, and shapes to ensure visual coherence. Audio tracks for guided interaction instructions and feedback sounds were gathered before starting the application development.

Unity 3D was used to create the application, which consists of six primary scenes: The Homepage, the Markers page, and four main scenes associated with objects. The Homepage is comprised solely of pre-existing GUI elements, which are linked to the other scenes and activate these scenes when the child clicks on them. The

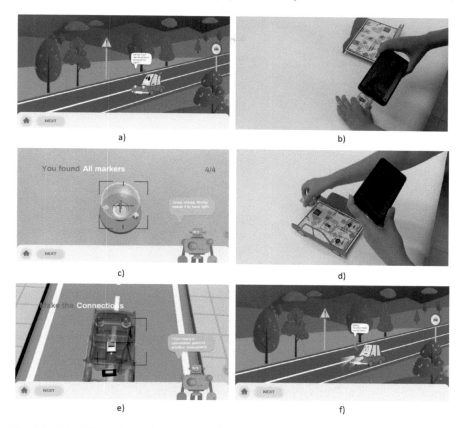

Fig. 6.11 The AR application's screenshots depict a scenario in which a problem is encountered with the car light being off. **a** The application prompts the child to locate the first element required to create the light circuit and solve the issue. **b** The child correctly selects the marker for the first element, which is the battery, and frames it. **c** Next, the child selects another necessary component, which is the lamp. **d** The application then instructs the child to arrange the components and **e** establish connections between them by choosing the virtual components displayed in AR. **f** Upon completing these steps accurately, the car's light system is restored to working order

four primary scenes, on the other hand, are more intricate and contain a variety of elements, including Graphical User Interface (GUI) elements, animations, video, and AR components that are triggered based on user interaction. Multiple scripts were created to manage AR interactions, with the primary script allowing the child to draw lines between circuit components by touching the device screen. When the child clicks on the first component, a small augmented pipe is created, which follows the orientation of the user's input on the screen and adjusts its length until the second component of the connection is reached. If the second component is not reached, the pipe is automatically removed, giving the child the opportunity

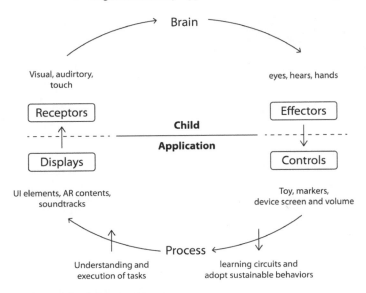

Fig. 6.12 Model representing the man–machine interactions

to perform the interaction again. Unity was used to create various animations that provide instructions and feedback about the child's actions.

Credits: Students: Sara Kashfi, Ava Aghali Tari, Julieta Grigiol, Marina Busato, Virtual and Physical Prototyping course, School of Design, Politecnico di Milano, Academic Year 20/21.

Video YouTube: https://youtu.be/Sf2D7p0BhYQ

6.3 Augmented Reality Application for Learning Plants' Biological Processes

Objective: Design an educational application that allows children to understand the entire lifespan of a plant and learn its scientific microscopic processes.

Description: In recent times, the integration of technology in subjects such as mathematics and science education has gained momentum due to its ability to foster students' engagement and comprehension of complex concepts. Science subjects are often challenging for students due to their use of abstract representations [11]. Augmented Reality has emerged as a promising tool to enhance science education by providing a more effective means of presenting abstract concepts that are difficult to visualize in traditional science lessons [12]. In contrast to conventional teaching methods, which often result in passive absorption of abstract scientific knowledge that may not be fully understood, AR in education enables students to actively experiment with scientific topics, thereby enhancing their motivation and learning outcomes. By applying AR technology to education, students can enjoy a more hands-on learning experience, which is particularly useful in exploring biological processes in plants.

Requirements: Here are the key criteria that must be met for the application's design:

- Ensuring the scientific accuracy of the presented materials;
- Incorporating interactive AR content;
- Providing visual and auditory components;
- Allowing for content updates and information status saving over time;
- Enabling the acquisition and analysis of real-world data to impact the AR content.

Concept: *Plant* is an AR application designed to enhance science education by providing a more engaging and interactive experience beyond traditional classroom lectures. The application enables students to gain a better understanding of the various biological processes that occur during a plant's lifespan, as well as how environmental factors can impact these processes. In the early elementary grades, children typically learn by interacting with the world around them using their senses. However, their understanding of scientific concepts can sometimes differ from that of the scientific community. Children may attempt to relate scientific explanations to their own life experiences, often anthropomorphizing processes without considering those that are imperceptible to the naked eye. In the realm of biology, a major challenge is the inability to observe biological processes that occur within a specific time frame or at the microscopic level. Despite this, it is important for primary school students to develop a foundational understanding of plants' biological processes and needs. Anderson et al. [13] as well as the National Science Frameworks [14] and the Next Generation Science Standards [15] emphasize that students in grades K-5 should possess basic knowledge of plants' growth, development, structure, and necessities, such as air, water, nutrients, and light. Additionally, students should recognize that plants can absorb nutrients from their surroundings and that changes in the environment can impact their survival. They should also understand that plants respond to external stimuli and that they require certain characteristics to thrive. With the advent of technology, digital-native students stand to benefit greatly from its integration into their learning experience.

The main objective of the *Plant* AR educational application is to educate students about the various biological processes that occur throughout a plant's lifespan. The application is intended for children between the ages of eight and ten, who are learning about plant biology for the first time. This age group has been selected as the primary user demographic because it is deemed the most appropriate in terms of both subject knowledge and digital literacy, thereby allowing for the full exploration of the application's technological capabilities.

Design: Children may encounter challenges when interacting with real plants, and even minor errors can have irreversible consequences on the plant's health. In addition to imparting basic plant knowledge, the *Plant* application also teaches children how to care for plants by demonstrating how external environmental factors can be controlled, and how this control affects the plant's biological processes. AR technology presents an effective alternative for fostering the curiosity of younger generations by enabling interaction in both the real and virtual worlds. This approach minimizes the risk of irreversible mistakes and allows for a trial-and-error approach to learning.

To develop the *Plant* application, an artificial plant was utilized as the foundation for the AR content. To simplify the content activation process, the plant was not employed as the AR marker. Instead, an image marker was printed and affixed to the vase containing the artificial plant, as depicted in Fig. 6.13.

Using the *Plant* application, children can observe the effects of different environmental conditions on the health of a real plant and gain insight into the otherwise invisible biological processes through AR technology. For instance, children can learn about the impact of varying light conditions and watering patterns on a plant. They can also observe the plant's lifecycle, including phases such as blooming, pollination, fruit growth, and new plant development. Figure 6.14 provides a visualization of some of the specific information that can be learned in each of these phases.

Fig. 6.13 Real artificial plant and the image marker used for the activation of the AR contents

FACTORS DETECTED	→	PLANT LIFECYCLE	→	LEARNING
• Light detection • Watering • Growing and pruning		• Blooming • Pollination • Fruit growth • New plant appearance		• Microscopic cycles • specific information on plant cycles

Fig. 6.14 Specific information that can be learned through the *Plant* application: environmental factors detected, plant lifecycle steps and learning elements

During the experience, the information is predominantly conveyed through the utilization of AR, utilizing both 3D objects and 2D Graphical User Interface (GUI) elements. The 3D objects serve to depict various aspects of the plant life cycle, including flowers, leaves, pollinators like bees, fruits, and emerging new plants. Furthermore, important processes such as photosynthesis and cellular respiration are visualized using three-dimensional representations of carbon dioxide and oxygen molecules. Additionally, interactive 3D tools like a watering can and scissors are provided to the children within the AR environment.

Throughout the experience, a friendly and approachable 2D character accompanies and guides children on how to perform the correct actions. The inclusion of this character aims to enhance engagement and facilitate understanding of the presented content. The character's tone of voice has been intentionally crafted to be informal and straightforward, creating a welcoming environment for the children.

The GUI incorporates a prominent feature known as the status bar, which visually represents the plant's parameters using rounded shapes and soft colors. This status bar can be accessed and displayed on top of other screen elements as needed. The interface buttons maintain a consistent green color scheme throughout the application, while other 2D elements and icons are depicted in white, as shown in Fig. 6.15.

To ensure the plant's survival, children are actively involved in engaging with it, and their actions directly impact the plant's life cycle. These interactions can take place either through direct manipulation of 3D models or through interactions with the 2D components of the GUI.

Technology: The development of the application utilized Unity 3D [1] as the primary platform. To integrate Augmented Reality content, the Vuforia SDK [16] and the AR Foundation Plugin were incorporated. Various Assets from the Unity Assets Store [3] were utilized to facilitate simple user interactions. Notably, the implementation of

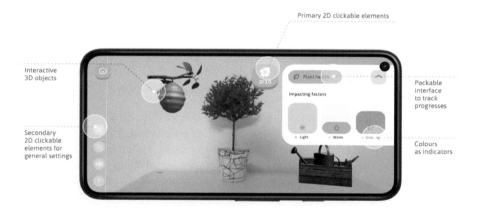

Fig. 6.15 Variety of interactive elements, including 3D objects, 2D graphics, and a graphical user interface (GUI), to engage and educate children offered in the *Plant* application

Lean Touch, Lean GUI, and Lean Transition Assets proved instrumental in achieving this objective.

For the creation of 3D models, Blender [17] was employed, while Adobe Illustrator was utilized to design the interface elements. This combination of tools allowed for the seamless integration of visually appealing and interactive elements within the application.

Architecture: The system architecture comprises the physical plant and the smartphone application. Figure 6.16 illustrates the interaction flow that outlines the various actions that the child must undertake to engage with both the physical plant and the AR content. As mentioned earlier, the child can observe the microscopic processes of the plant, take care of it, and acquire new knowledge during the experience. The primary objective is to relocate the physical plant to diverse environments to initiate two biological processes of the plant—photosynthesis and cellular respiration-, which are made visible in AR.

Additionally, the child is encouraged to engage in virtual watering of the plant, which serves to enhance their understanding of the appropriate amount of water required and the consequences of over or under-watering. Through the implementation of Augmented Reality, the child can also delve into the 3D model of the plant and explore various scientific concepts. Each action taken by the child has a direct impact on the plant's condition, which is visually reflected through different effects in the AR environment. For example, insufficient watering leads to changes in leaf color and gradual withering of the plant. On the contrary, when the plant is thriving, its flowers blossom, fruits mature, and new plants emerge as the fruits naturally fall to the ground.

At the start of the journey, a concise tutorial provides an introduction to the key interactions that will take place during the experience. Then, the initial interaction stage entails scanning the marker to activate the AR content. Upon scanning the physical plant with a smartphone, the first screen provides an overview of the actions to be carried out during the experience, depicted through a 2D character. The first task involves dragging the water to the plant, using a 3D watering can, to provide it with the required water. The moisture level of the soil is indicated on the plant's status bar, linked to the plant's water status. Once the plant attains a healthy state and is prepared to blossom, the child is prompted to click a button that randomly generates flowers on the foliage (Fig. 6.17).

When the plant is ready for pollination, the child can click on a 3D bee and drag it onto the flowers to initiate the process. Following pollination, fruits start to appear on the plant, and when they are ripe, the child can shake the smartphone to scatter the seeds and allow new plants to grow. Additionally, by selecting specific elements of the new-born plant, the child can explore its anatomy, including nodes, leaves, and flowers. They can observe these components up close and gain an understanding of how leaf veins connect to the plant's stem, facilitating nutrient transportation throughout the plant. With regards to flowers, the child can learn about the protective functions of petals in supporting the blooming process.

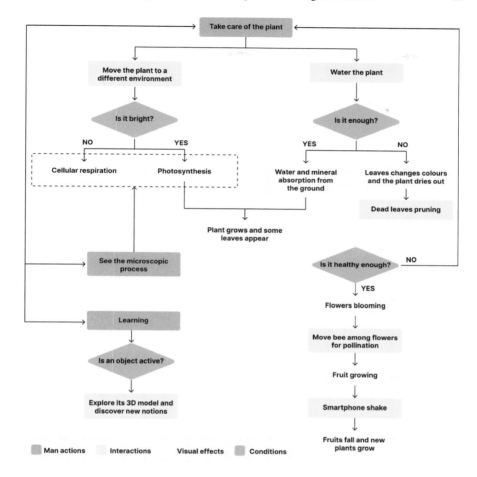

Fig. 6.16 Interaction flow of the *Plant* application

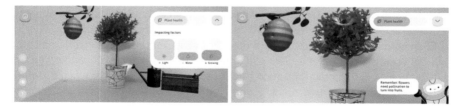

Fig. 6.17 Screenshots depicting the watering process and the blooming of the plant in the application

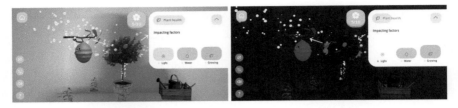

Fig. 6.18 Screenshots showcasing the plant's photosynthesis process during both day and night in the application

Throughout the experience, the child has the option to care for the plant by removing yellowish leaves and withered flowers whenever necessary. They can achieve this by selecting a 3D model of scissors and dragging it onto the plant canopy. Furthermore, the interface displays continuous monitoring of the plant's health through bars indicating the light, water, and growth levels. Of these parameters, the environmental light has a significant impact on the AR content, illustrating the plant's photosynthesis process during the day and night, as illustrated in Fig. 6.18.

Implementation: The initial phase of developing the AR application involved defining the image marker to ensure optimal recognition using the Vuforia SDK [16] plugin. Instead of using the actual plant itself, an image attached to the plant vase was chosen as the marker to simplify the tracking system. This approach allows the AR educational app to be used with different real plants by simply attaching the image to various vases without being limited to a specific plant type.

The next step involved creating the 3D models using Blender [17], a 3D modeling software, and designing the 2D GUI using Adobe Illustrator. Once the assets were ready, a Unity project was created, and all the 3D and 2D elements were imported into the project. Additionally, the Vuforia plugin was added, and various AR-related aspects were configured, including the creation of the image marker library.

Within the Unity project, several scenes were developed to correspond to different phases of the plant life cycle. To bring these scenes to life, 3D models were utilized to create various animations within Unity. These animations were then connected to a single Unity Animator Controller, which was created for each scene. To enhance the visual appeal, particle effects were incorporated into the animations.

Each animation is triggered within the Animator Controller by detecting a collision between two 3D objects. The occurrence of this collision is dependent on the child's choices and interactions during the experience. For instance, when the child pours water into the virtual plant, a collision between the water and the plant is detected, subsequently triggering the flower blooming animation.

The integration of object interactions, such as dragging, clicking, and pinching, was achieved by incorporating external Assets called Lean Touch and Lean Transition. These Assets enabled the seamless integration of these interactions into the AR application. Upon performing an interaction, the corresponding animation is triggered and displayed. Simultaneously, the GUI is updated to provide accurate information about the plant's status and health conditions. To enhance the visual experience, the GUI incorporates transition animations, which were implemented using the Lean GUI Asset. These animations add fluidity and polish to the GUI elements as they appear or transition between states.

To accurately represent the biological processes of photosynthesis and respiration, a distinct approach was taken. Instead of being triggered by specific user interactions, the animations depicting 3D carbon dioxide and oxygen molecules are influenced by the ambient light conditions in which the child is immersed during the experience. This approach was chosen to ensure a more realistic representation of the biological processes.

The environmental light detection relies on the camera of the device and is facilitated by the AR foundation plugin. This feature enables the application to estimate the current light conditions in the environment. The extracted light values are then utilized to dynamically control the emission and direction of the 3D particle animations showcased in the AR experience. Specifically, the respiration animation is triggered when the detected light value is low, while the photosynthesis animation is activated when a high light value is detected.

In addition to the primary interactions previously discussed, there is another interaction that offers a unique experience for the children. By shaking the smartphone device, the child can simulate the action of fruits falling onto the soil, which subsequently generates a new plant. This interaction leverages the motion sensors present in the smartphone and is implemented by monitoring the device's inputs through a Unity script. This feature adds an element of physical engagement and interactivity, enhancing the overall immersive experience for the child.

Credits: Students: Chiara Libralon, Sharon Manfredi, Wenbo Yang, Virtual and Physical Prototyping course, School of Design, Politecnico di Milano, Academic Year 21/22.

Video Youtube: https://youtu.be/6bB1lSj-E9s

References

1. Unity 3D. https://unity.com/. Last accessed 15 May 2023
2. Unity-MARS. https://unity.com/products/unity-mars. Last accessed 15 May 2023
3. Unity Asset Store. https://assetstore.unity.com/. Last accessed 15 May 2023
4. Rhinoceros, https://www.rhino3d.com/it/, Last accessed 15 May 2023
5. Karagozlu D (2021) Creating a sustainable education environment with augmented reality technology. Sustainability 13(11):5851
6. Lucas P, Vaca D, Dominguez F, Ochoa X (2018) Virtual circuits: an augmented reality circuit simulator for engineering students. In: 2018 IEEE 18th international conference on advanced learning technologies (ICALT), pp 380–384
7. Baldé CP, Forti V, Gray V, Kuehr R, Stegmann P (2017) The global e-waste monitor 2017: quantities, flows and resources. United Nations University, International Telecommunication Union, and International Solid Waste Association
8. Gelman DL (2014) Design for kids: digital products for playing and learning. Rosenfeld Media

9. Poelman WA (2005) Technology diffusion in product design-Towards an integration of technology diffusion in the design process. TUDelft PhD thesis, 2005, https://repository.tudelft.nl/islandora/object/uuid%3Ad9850382-00c6-4f16-ab3f-3336aa39df01. Last accessed 15 May 2023
10. Figma. https://www.figma.com. Last accessed 15 May 2023
11. Palmer DH (1999) Exploring the link between students' scientific and nonscientific conceptions. Sci Educ 83(6):639–653
12. Arvanitis TN, Petrou A, Knight JF, Savas S, Sotiriou S, Gargalakos M, Gialouri E (2009) Human factors and qualitative pedagogical evaluation of a mobile augmented reality system for science education used by learners with physical disabilities. Pers Ubiquit Comput 13(3):243–250
13. Anderson JL, Ellis JP, Jones AM (2014) Understanding early elementary children's conceptual knowledge of plant structure and function through drawings. CBE Life Sci Educ Fall 13(3):375–386
14. NRC (2012) A framework for science education. National Academies Press, Washington, DC
15. Next generation science standards: for states, by states. National Academies Press, Washington, DC. https://www.achieve.org/next-generation-science-standards. Last accessed 15 May 2023
16. Vuforia SDK. https://developer.vuforia.com/downloads/SDK. Last accessed 15 May 2023
17. Blender. https://www.blender.org/. Last accessed 15 May 2023

Chapter 7
Applications of Multisensory Experiences in eXtended Reality

Abstract This chapter presents three examples demonstrating the advantages of multisensory experiences in eXtended Reality applications. The first case study involves a training application designed to familiarize users with laboratory machinery, incorporating the senses of sight, hearing, and smell. The second case study concerns the utilization of multisensory experiences in Augmented Reality to facilitate language learning and enhance the exploration of a new city. The third one concerns a multisensory application including visual components, sounds, and odors for learning music.

7.1 Virtual Reality for Training Safe Use of Machinery

Objective: Create and develop a multisensory Virtual Reality experience intended to educate operators on the proper utilization of industrial machinery and the corresponding safety guidelines.

Description: Training operators in the usage of specific machinery is a crucial consideration in various industries, as well as in contexts like university laboratories that require proficiency in operating machinery. Currently, operators typically acquire their skills through hands-on experience and on-the-job training, supplemented by manuals outlining best practices. However, this approach can be time-consuming, resource-intensive, and potentially hazardous due to the operators' lack of experience. To address these challenges, Virtual Reality (VR) technology can be employed to simulate the industrial environment and enhance operator training. By leveraging VR, immersive multisensory experiences can be created, aiding in the comprehension and retention of essential tasks during training sessions. Based on this premise, a case study has been conducted at Politecnico di Milano, where a university laboratory houses numerous industrial machines. The study focuses on designing and developing a VR application that offers a multisensory experience to train operators on the usage of specific machinery and the importance of wearing Personal Protective Equipment (PPE) for safety purposes.

Requirements: The design of the application entails several key requirements, which are as follows:

- incorporate olfactory stimulation as part of the multisensory experience;
- establish an immersive training environment;
- emphasize usability aspects to assist users throughout the experience;
- offer a user-friendly and easily navigable interface;
- deliver clear feedback regarding the operator's actions.

Concept: Training involves acquiring the necessary skills to operate machinery effectively, control it, and handle challenging situations with utmost safety. Virtual Reality has gained widespread adoption in industrial training due to its ability to simulate risky or impractical scenarios in a safe and controlled environment [1]. VR training is particularly valuable in the manufacturing sector, where it is extensively utilized for tasks such as industrial maintenance [2, 3] and assembly [4, 5]. However, VR training can also be advantageous in various other settings that involve the use of specific machinery, such as university laboratories. In these environments, it is crucial to learn the precise procedures for operating each machine and to understand the corresponding PPE requirements. Wearing appropriate PPE, including gloves, masks, and goggles, is essential for minimizing exposure to dangerous situations while working with machinery. The presented VR application focuses on providing multisensory training for operating the machinery found within a university laboratory. Users can explore the laboratory, select individual machines, and learn the specific actions to perform, as well as the necessary PPE to wear during operation. To enhance the training experience, the application incorporates olfactory stimulation alongside visual and auditory cues. The introduction of smell helps engage the user during explanations of the required tasks and provides positive or negative feedback based on their actions. By completing training on all the machines within the virtual environment, the user can successfully conclude the entire experience and become eligible for access to the real laboratory.

Design: The VR application follows a User-Centered Design (UCD) approach [6], where the user actively participates in the design process. In this case, the students involved in developing the application also serve as the target users, as they have previously received training on the machines found in the university laboratory. Their familiarity with the tasks associated with operating the real machines enables them to offer valuable suggestions and insights to enhance the training experience. To create the virtual experience, a 3D recreation of the actual Prototyping Laboratory in the Design Department of Politecnico di Milano was developed. The machines and tools within the laboratory were realistically designed to provide users with an immersive training experience. The laboratory consists of two distinct rooms housing various machines, including the Band saw, Lathe, Disc Sander, Press Drill, Press Paint Station, Foam Cutter, and Fire Extinguisher.

The objective of the VR application is to successfully complete the training for all the machines and obtain certification for their operation. To assist users in tracking their progress, a Graphical User Interface (GUI) is utilized. The GUI serves as a visual

Fig. 7.1 Diagram
illustrating the virtual
training process for a single
machine

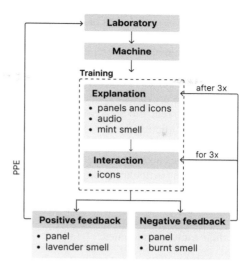

reminder, indicating which machines the user has already completed training on and which machines are yet to be experienced. The training experience is illustrated in Fig. 7.1.

At the beginning of the training experience, an overview of the safety rules and tasks involved is provided to the user. This introductory phase ensures that the user is familiar with the necessary precautions and objectives before commencing the training. Once equipped with this knowledge, the user is granted the freedom to explore the virtual environment and initiate the training by selecting a specific machine of interest. The training itself is divided into two distinct parts. In the first part, a comprehensive explanation is delivered, detailing the specific tasks that need to be performed. This instructional phase aims to provide the user with a clear understanding of the procedures and actions required. During the instructional phase, information is presented through both audio narration and text displayed via GUI panels. To assist the user in focusing their attention, GUI icons are utilized to represent the necessary PPE and machine components that require emphasis during the explanation and interaction stages. In the second part, the user is actively engaged and prompted to interact with the various components of the machine, as well as the corresponding PPE. This hands-on interaction allows for practical application and reinforces the learning process. During the instructional phase, a subtle mint fragrance is released through a device named Olfactory Display (OD) to enhance user engagement and stimulation. The choice of mint scent is based on scientific findings demonstrating its ability to arouse the central nervous system [7], leading to increased attention and alertness [8].

Once the user successfully completes all the designated tasks, they have the opportunity to activate the machine and simulate its real usage. At this crucial stage, the training outcome is accompanied by feedback that reinforces the user's performance. Throughout the user's training with each machine, both the VR application and the

OD provide outputs based on the user's specific inputs, as depicted in Table 7.1. At the beginning of training with each machine, the user engages with the VR application, simultaneously receiving auditory and visual information through animations while experiencing the activating scent of mint emitted by the OD. Subsequently, the user is required to correctly select the machine components and appropriate PPE based on the previous explanation. Each time an element is selected, an animation replicates its realistic behavior.

After completing the necessary actions, the user proceeds to activate the machine. At this stage, the application provides feedback on the training outcome through an animation, accompanied by the OD delivering either a pleasant or unpleasant fragrance. In particular, to augment the feedback experience, two distinct scents are employed: lavender is emitted as a positive indicator of successful training, while the unpleasant smell of a burnt-out candle signifies an unsuccessful attempt. This multisensory approach enhances the feedback and reinforces the user's understanding of their training outcomes.

Technology: The VR application is specifically designed for use with a Head Mounted Display (HMD) and incorporates a wearable Olfactory Display (OD) that is integrated into the HMD through an Arduino board [9]. The OD, which utilizes the piezoelectric technique, is seamlessly incorporated based on [10] to provide the user with the ability to experience three distinct odors during the training. The VR application is developed using Unity 3D [11], with the implementation of VR functionalities and interactions facilitated by the integration of the Open XR Plugin [12].

Architecture: The system architecture, which is illustrated in Fig. 7.2 consists of the VR application, which is delivered through the Meta Quest 2 headset [13], and the Olfactory Display, capable of delivering three distinct fragrances.

The MetaQuest and its controllers track the user's movements and interactions, triggering several elements in the VR environments (such as animations) and send input to the OD to deliver the fragrances.

Implementation: Within the Unity project, multiple scenes were constructed to represent the laboratory environment and individual rooms dedicated to each

Table 7.1 User interactions, VR application, and the olfactory display outputs generated during machine training

Input	Output	
User	Application	Olfactory display
Hear and read the information Smell the odor	Deliver the explanation animation	Release the odor
Select the machine components and PPEs	Display animation based on selected elements	
Start the machine	Provide feedback regarding the training outcomes	Release the pleasant or unpleasant odor

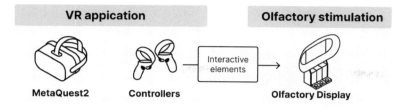

Fig. 7.2 System architecture of the VR multisensory application

machine. These scenes were interconnected, and a basic script was implemented to load each scene based on specific user input. The Opens XR Plugin facilitated the implementation of VR movements and interactions, which were controlled using the MetaQuest controllers. The development of the environment began by creating 3D models that accurately represent the laboratory and the machinery within it, including all the main components of the machines. Each scene was then equipped with various animations that were connected using the Unity animator. These animations were controlled by a script and triggered based on the user's interactions during the training. Additionally, a Graphical User Interface (GUI) was designed using Adobe Illustrator and incorporated into the Unity project. The GUI was implemented to assist and guide the user throughout the training process. Panels and icons were utilized to highlight interactive elements and provide feedback to the user (Fig. 7.3).

Regarding the multisensory stimulation, voice audio and sounds have been incorporated to aid in content explanation and provide feedback for the user's actions, such as selecting an element. Furthermore, the delivery of three different odors has been achieved through the integration of the Olfactory Display device. The Olfactory Display, as shown in Fig. 7.4, has been specifically designed and built, taking inspiration from the device described in the referenced work [10].

The OD device consists of three piezoelectric components and corresponding liquid fragrance containers. These components were created through 3D printing, using a reference kit as a starting point [14]. The OD device is attached to the front of the Meta Quest headset to ensure direct delivery of the scents to the user's nose. Each piezoelectric component is connected to an Arduino board and is individually activated based on the virtual experience to deliver the specific scent. Serial communication between Unity and Arduino is established using various scripts, enabling the transmission of input from Unity and the subsequent activation of the piezoelectric components upon receiving signals from Arduino.

Credits: Students: Nicola Besana and Giuseppe Fazio, Virtual and Physical Prototyping course, School of Design, Politecnico di Milano, Academic Year 19/20.

Video Youtube: https://youtu.be/cEnyCHSBNJg

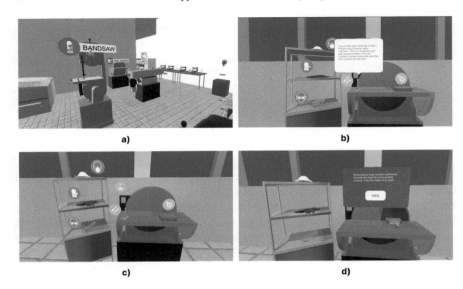

Fig. 7.3 Screenshots showcasing the graphical user interface (GUI) in the VR application for virtual training: **a** The virtual depiction of the laboratory and machinery. **b** The instructional phase of the disk sander training. **c** The interactive phase of the training where the user interacts with the disk sander. **d** Feedback provided to the user regarding the training outcome, with the option to retry the interactive phase in case of a negative result

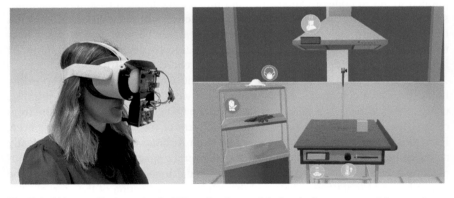

Fig. 7.4 Olfactory display and unity VR application used during the foam cutter training to enhance the user experience

7.2 eXtended Reality for Learning Languages

Objective: Design and develop an Augmented Reality multisensory experience with the aim of enhancing language learning and assisting in the exploration of a new city.

Description: Numerous studies have shown the significant advantages of learning foreign languages during youth. These benefits include the enhancement of cognitive and memory skills, improved interpersonal communication abilities, the development of independent problem-solving skills, and increased self-esteem. However, the study of new languages can sometimes prove challenging and monotonous for teenagers, particularly with traditional educational methods. Integrating digital technologies for educational purposes, when fully harnessed, can foster engaging learning experiences and facilitate student progress.

The objective of the case study is to develop a multisensory Augmented Reality (AR) application that enables teenagers to learn a new language while engaging in a playful and creative exploration of a foreign city. The study incorporates olfactory stimulation to enhance concentration and stimulate memory functions, considering the profound impact on emotional aspects as well as various psychological and physiological conditions. The project specifically concentrates on the city of London and the acquisition of the English language.

Requirements: the application requirements encompass the following:

- delivering a multisensory experience to enhance learning performance,
- designing an easily accessible and user-friendly interface,
- creating an aesthetically pleasing environment,
- allowing customization options for young users.

Concept: In recent times, numerous studies have been dedicated to exploring innovative teaching methodologies [15, 16], particularly tailored to meet the unique characteristics and requirements of the current generation of digital natives. Notably, certain studies have demonstrated that employing new technologies in educational tools yields significant long-term outcomes [17, 18]. Regarding educational research on language acquisition, there is a strong consensus that learning languages during childhood and adolescence is more advantageous and can yield numerous long-term benefits [19, 20]. However, employing conventional methods such as in-person lessons, textbooks, and intensive courses for language learning can prove challenging and uninteresting for teenagers. The cohort of digital natives constitutes a distinct user segment with unique characteristics and requirements, and their preferences and needs are greatly influenced by the rapid proliferation of new technologies.

As a result, it becomes necessary to update traditional teaching methods to accommodate new requirements. One prominent challenge in this domain is the decreasing attention spans observed among children. Consequently, there is a need to conceive and implement novel approaches that captivate their interest and foster a desire to learn. Hence, educational practices that emphasize playfulness, creativity, and hands-on experiences are being developed [21].

Students are no longer passive recipients of knowledge but are required to assume an active and purposeful role in embracing new problem-solving and project-based learning methodologies. Clearly, this necessitates leveraging the interactive and diverse potential offered by emerging technologies. Built upon the foundations of immersion and interactivity, eXtended Reality (XR) technologies have the potential to captivate students' curiosity, leading to more active engagement in their learning [22, 23].

While visual stimulation remains the predominant approach when integrating these technologies, efforts are being made to explore new learning methodologies that engage multiple senses, particularly the sense of smell. Odors have the ability to impact various profound aspects of individuals' lives, such as evoking memories, influencing mood (relieving stress or enhancing calmness), and playing a pivotal role in decision-making [24].

Drawing upon these principles, the *City Flavour* application has been created to offer a unique experience wherein AR elements are superimposed onto the physical map of London (Fig. 7.5), and corresponding scents are introduced based on different locations marked on the map. In this case study, specific fragrances have been carefully chosen to enhance the stimulation of mnemonic faculties during language studies and to facilitate the practical application of acquired knowledge in real-life situations.

Design: The *City Flavor* application comprises a kit featuring a paper map of London, the focal city of exploration, along with a case containing eight scented capsules and an Olfactory Display device. The map is divided into seven zones, serving as image markers for activating the AR features. Within each zone, there are four points of attraction categorized into eight distinct categories, including must-see locations,

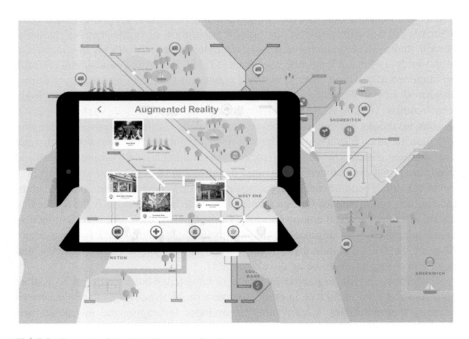

Fig. 7.5 Concept of the *City Flavor* application

food establishments, cultural sites, coffee shops, emergency services, bars, transportation hubs, and shopping destinations. Each category is associated with a specific scent, enhancing the learning and memorization process. The chosen scents include citrus, bread, cinnamon, coffee, lemon, bergamot, mint, and vanilla. The selection of scents was based on their inherent characteristics and the potential stimulation effects they can provide when combined. Moreover, the combinations were carefully considered, taking into account the psychological and physiological influences of particular odor types, which offer various benefits [25]. The connection between odors, categories, and expected effects is illustrated in Table 7.2.

The teenager can utilize the AR application on a tablet and connect the Olfactory Display device to the tablet for a comprehensive experience. Upon framing the desired area for exploration, AR polaroid pictures showcasing images and addresses of selected locations emerge on the points of interest marked on the map (Fig. 7.6). Subsequently, users can choose a specific category of interest and access a collection of helpful English expressions pertinent to various everyday life situations. By pressing a button, the corresponding scent associated with the chosen category is emitted from the Olfactory Display device. Each category offers six useful sentences, allowing users to study them, read their translations, and listen to correct pronunciation in the foreign language.

Technology: The *City Flavour* application has been created as AR tablet application using Unity 3D [9], with the integration of the Vuforia SDK [26] to incorporate the AR functionalities. Additionally, an Olfactory Display device employing a fan-based technique has been integrated to deliver eight different scents.

Architecture: The system architecture consists of multiple components, including the tablet-based AR application, the Olfactory Display equipped with four fans, and a set of eight capsule fragrances (Fig. 7.7). The Olfactory Display is a desktop device specifically designed to be connected to the tablet.

Implementation: the initial step in the implementation process involved ensuring the reliable recognition of the image marker for accurate detection through the tablet's

Table 7.2 Combination of categories, odors, and effects

Categories	Odours	Physiological/Psychological effects
Must see	Citrus	Feelings of positivity and tranquility
Food	Bread	Taste stimulation
Culture	Cinnamon	Cognitive functions and concentration levels
Coffee	Coffee	Invigorating effect. Odor capable of overriding previous olfactory sensations
Emergency	Lemon	Levels of attention and tranquility
Bars	Bergamotto	Good moods and happiness
Transports	Mint	Levels of attentiveness and responsiveness
Shopping	Vanilla	Feelings of enjoyment and relaxation

Fig. 7.6 AR elements present in the *City Flavour* application displayed as digital polaroid pictures overlaid onto the physical map

Fig. 7.7 Schematic representation illustrating the application including the tablet, the Olfactory Display, and the fragrances

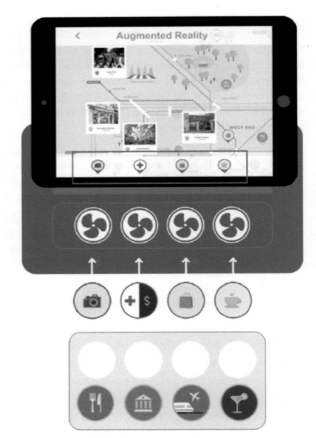

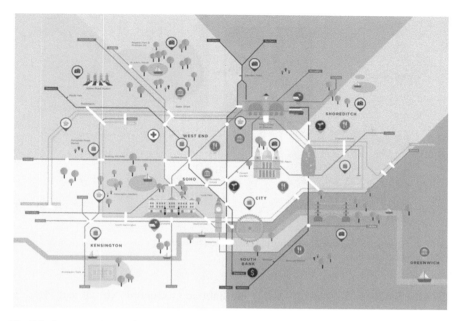

Fig. 7.8 Image marker utilized for AR tracking purposes

camera. Various map solutions were designed, employing different strategies such as incorporating distinct contrasts and avoiding symmetries and patterns. The graphic components of the application were designed using various software from the Adobe suite, including Illustrator, InDesign, and Photoshop, and then imported into the Unity application. Figure 7.8 showcases the final image marker that was utilized.

The second phase involved the development of interactions and animations within the AR application. Additionally, audio tracks to support the learning activity were recorded and imported into the Unity project.

In the final step, the implementation of the Olfactory Display took place. The Olfactory Display is comprised of a case containing an Arduino board [13] and four fans (40 × 40 × 10 mm, 12 V) where the scented capsules are positioned during application usage to facilitate the emission of specific odors (Fig. 7.9).

The fragrant capsules consist of cotton disks that have been saturated with various liquid aromas, each offering a distinct fragrance. The Olfactory Display is governed by an Arduino board, which is connected to the AR tablet through a USB-C cable. The start and stop inputs are managed by scripts that establish a connection between the AR application and the Arduino board. The electronic board comprises four separate switch transistors, with each transistor activating a specific fan based on the input received from the application.

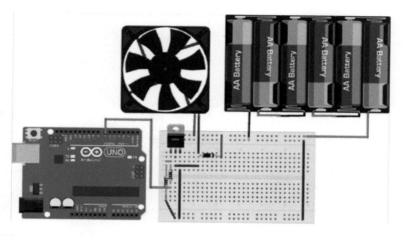

Fig. 7.9 Schematic diagram illustrating the connection between a fan and the Arduino board, along with the associated components

Credits: Students: Rossana Mascioli and Sabrina Occhialini, Virtual and Physical Prototyping course, School of Design, Politecnico di Milano, Academic Year 19/20.

Video Youtube: https://youtu.be/UXLA15h7Wno

7.3 eXtended Reality Application for Learning Music

Objective: create a multi-sensorial experience that is memorable, interactive and challenging for kids, with educational purposes related to the music world.

Description: The music education program at school often provides opportunities for children to select an instrument to learn in class. However, due to limited time and traditional teaching methods, some students struggle to fully master the instrument and lose motivation to continue their musical education. As a result, parents may be hesitant to purchase the instrument for their child without assurance of continued interest and dedication. Thus, the aim of this project is to create an Augmented Reality (AR) musical application that engages children in a playful and multisensory approach to music education, eliminating the need for immediate instrument purchase. Additionally, the application should enhance students' motivation and enthusiasm towards learning their chosen instrument.

Requirements: The following are the key criteria that must be met for the application's design:

- easy and cheap access to learning musical instruments in the education context;
- stimulating the students to grow their interest in learning music through fun and amusement and supporting memorization;

Solfeggio syllable	DO	RE	MI	FA	SOL	LA	SI
Color code NCS	S1080-R	S0585-Y60R	S0580-Y	S1075-G50Y	S1565	S2060-R70B	S2060-R30B
Hue	●	●	●	●	●	●	●

Fig. 7.10 Color music notation system used in *MozAR*

- engaging kids with the content through manual manipulation of tangible items and not only through digital interaction;
- challenging the students to progress in their knowledge and learn more gradually.

Concept: *MozAR* is an Augmented Reality application designed to teach the fundamentals of music to children. The application offers support in reading notes on sheet music and playing them on a range of instruments. Additionally, the application employs the use of olfactory feedback for a multisensory experience that enhances content retention.

To fulfill these objectives, *MozAR* includes a variety of features, such as:

- variety of virtual instruments that can be played;
- color associations with notes for synesthetic learning [27];
- physical markers for interaction with music-related elements, such as instruments, notes, and pentagrams;
- increasing level of difficulty as children progress through the application.

The concept of connecting colors and musical notes has been explored in individuals with chromesthesia, where sounds can produce visual colors. Studies have shown that certain notes consistently evoke particular color tones [28, 29]. Various color music notation systems combining colors and written musical notes have been developed to aid young music learners [30–32], such as the method presented in Fig. 7.10, which is the one utilized in the *MozAR* app. This system was created by Kuo and Chuang [30] and links the wavelengths of colors to the pitch frequencies of sounds [32].

Design: The *MozAR* application was designed as a kit consisting of tangible components, including a set of markers, a cardboard platform for supporting the markers, and a scent diffuser, named Olfactory Display (OD) featuring two fragrances: lavender and rosemary. During use, an LED light included in the OD illuminates in pink and green hues to provide feedback to the user. The set of markers represent notes, instruments, and a pentagram and have been printed on cardboard cards that are easy to handle. These component are intended for children to engage with and learn musical concepts by playing. Each note is accompanied by a designated marker, illustrated in Fig. 7.11.

These notes are differentiated by a number, color, position on the pentagram, and a solfege hand gesture to assist with on-pitch singing, as displayed in Fig. 7.12.

To allow for customizable instrument selection, six markers were created for the user to choose from: piano, violin, flute, harp, guitar, and electric guitar (Fig. 7.13). The Logic Pro app [33] was utilized to record the sounds of each note for each

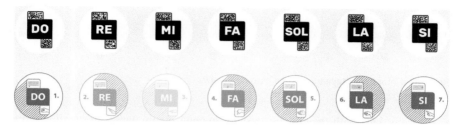

Fig. 7.11 Markers associated with notes

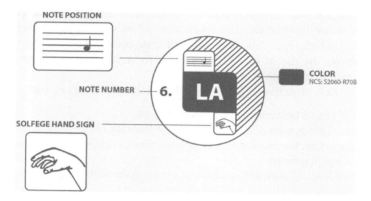

Fig. 7.12 Information associated with each note

instrument. Additionally, a group of markers was created for the selection of the pentagram.

The application is intended to be utilized on a mobile device, preferably a tablet, which allows for easy placement of support on a surface. This enables the user to use both hands to engage with the content. Additionally, prior to starting the experience, the user must connect and position the OD next to the mobile device in a visible location.

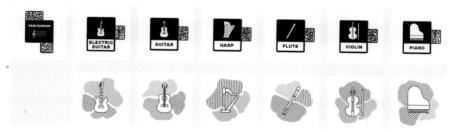

Fig. 7.13 Markers used for the selection of the instrument

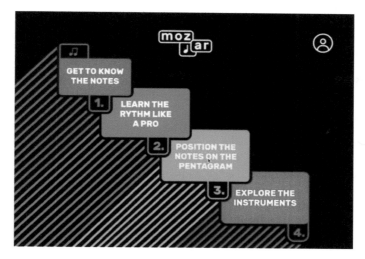

Fig. 7.14 User flow diagram

The application includes four functions (Fig. 7.14):

- Get to know the notes;
- Learn the rhythm like a pro;
- Position the notes on the pentagram;
- Explore the instruments.

Using these functions, the user can perform the following exercises:

- Mimic the solfege hand sound;
- Understand notes and rests values and durations;
- Drag and drop the digital notes onto the proper position of the pentagram;
- Play the different notes by using physical inputs.

Technology: The application has been implemented using the following technology:

- Unity for interface and 2D element integration;
- Vuforia for AR implementation;
- an Olfactory Display that emits two fragrances (rosemary and lavender) to induce relaxation or activate precision and velocity during exercise. Additionally, the OD features an LED light that changes color from pink to green based on the user's performance. The OD's shells were 3D printed, and was programmed with an Arduino board.

Architecture: The central hub for accessing the four exercises is the application homepage. Upon selecting one of the four menu items, a GUI pop-up appears and provides information on the chosen exercise and the necessary preparatory work. To successfully complete the AR exercises, specific markers must be prepared and correctly positioned in front of the camera. Following the instructions, the user can perform the exercise and receive both visual and olfactory feedback upon successful completion. In the event of an unsuccessful attempt, negative feedback is given only visually through the GUI and olfactory display light.

The initial activity aims to introduce the user to musical notes and solfege signs, utilizing marker notes. Upon identifying the corresponding marker for a note, the interface displays the appropriate hand gesture for the solfege sign and requests the user to replicate it before the camera.

In the second exercise, the focus shifts to time values and note durations, including rests. By scanning the singular note marker, the user can comprehend the note value and duration and then test their rhythm and acquired knowledge. The interface showcases whole, half, and quarter notes and rests, and the user can easily differentiate durations through accompanying soundtracks. Then, an AR bar demonstrates a sequence of notes and rest values adjacent to the marker. Once ready, the user can press and hold a button on the interface, following the bar's duration values accordingly. Pushing the button triggers the filling of the AR bar and the reproduction of a note sound. The user receives assistance in finding the correct rhythm through a micrometer sound and visual representation on the interface. As the exercise is quick, the accuracy of execution is only provided through visual feedback, and the user can repeat the exercise as many times as desired.

In the third exercise, the user must scan the pentagram marker to access an AR interface displaying the pentagram and notes in a line. The user must drag notes to fill empty spots on the pentagram (Fig. 7.15). If a note is placed incorrectly, it returns to the starting position. Correctly placed notes trigger positive visual and olfactory feedback, using the lavender fragrance.

During the final exercise, users are given the opportunity to experiment with the sounds generated by a variety of instruments. To begin, the user must arrange markers related to musical notes on the cardboard platform being used for support. After this, they can select an instrument and scan the corresponding marker. Once an instrument has been chosen, the cardboard platform can be framed to display AR representations of the notes. By interacting with the AR content, the user can listen to the sound of the selected instrument playing the specific note.

Implementation: Initially, Adobe Illustrator was utilized to design the application interface elements such as icons, illustrations, markers, cardboard platform, and 2D images related to the AR contents. To maintain consistency, the same style of colors and fonts were used, while ensuring adherence to the adopted colors music notation system. Subsequently, Logic Pro software [33] was used to create soundtracks for different musical notes and instruments.

Once these elements were completed, Unity 3D and Vuforia SDK were used to develop the AR application. The Unity project consists of five scenes, with the first scene featuring the application homepage that connects to four other scenes containing exercises that activate various contents depending on the marker scanned by the user.

The design and prototype of the Olfactory Display have been completed. It has a compact, rounded shape, as depicted in Fig. 7.16. The diffusor shells were created

Fig. 7.15 User positions notes and rests on the AR pentagram

with Rhinoceros software, then 3D printed. The inner shell contains two compartments for the lavender and rosemary fragrances, as well as a space for an Arduino board and related components for both the OD and LED light. Two piezoelectric sensors were used to create the OD's odor delivery module, one for each fragrance. Finally, Arduino was connected to Unity to control the LED lights and the piezoelectric sensor activation. Detailed instructions on how to create your own Olfactory Display can be retrieved in [10].

The integration of the OD into the AR application is performed by establishing a Serial communication between Unity and Arduino. As mentioned, the fragrances and the LED lights are adopted during the experience to support users during the exercises with the purpose of activating and relaxing them. During the exercises, two defined values, "v" and "g," are sent from Unity to Arduino to activate the two piezoelectric and the LED light contained inside the OD. The values are sent asynchronously, depending on the exercise performed. The "v" value is sent from the application, the pink light is activated, and the lavender fragrance is released. On the other hand, when the "g" value is sent from the application, the green light is activated, and the OD emits the rosemary fragrance (Fig. 7.17).

Credits: Students: Tala Chehade, Michela Alessandrello, Sara Andreani, Virtual and Physical Prototyping course, School of Design, Politecnico di Milano, Academic Year 19/20.

Video Youtube: https://youtu.be/w1v-RcPk_Zo

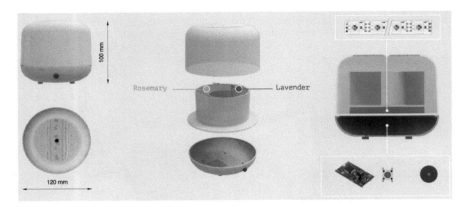

Fig. 7.16 Olfactory display used to deliver rosemary and lavender fragrances

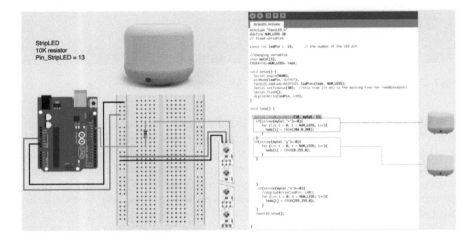

Fig. 7.17 Arduino coding to connect the OD with the AR application to control the LED light

References

1. Makranskya G, Borre-Gude S, Mayer RE (2019) Motivational and cognitive benefits of training in immersive virtual reality based on multiple assessments. Comput Assist Learn 35:691–707
2. Perez-Ramirez M, Arroyo-Figueroa G, Ayala A (2019) The use of a virtual reality training system to improve technical skill in the maintenance of live-line power distribution networks. Interact Learn Environ
3. Gavish N, Gutiérrez T, Webel S, Rodríguez J, Peveri M, Bockholt U, Tecchia M (2015) Evaluating virtual reality and augmented reality training for industrial maintenance and assembly tasks. Interact Learn Environ 23(6):778–798
4. Abidi MH, Al-Ahmari A, Ahmad A, Ameen W, Alkhalefah H (2019) Assessment of virtual reality-based manufacturing assembly training system. Int J Adv Manuf Technol 105:3743–3759

5. Roldán J, Crespo E, Martín-Barrio A, Peña-Tapia E, Barrientos A (2019) A training system for Industry 4.0 operators in complex assemblies based on virtual reality and process mining. Robot Comput Integr Manuf 59:305–316
6. Abras C, Maloney-Krichmar D, Preece J (2004) User-centered design. In: Bainbridge W (ed) Encyclopedia of human-computer interaction. Sage Publications, Thousand Oaks. 37(4), 445–456
7. Warm JS, Dember WN, Parasuraman R (1991) Effects of olfactory stimulation on performance and stress in a visual sustained attention task. J Soc Cosmet Chem 42:199–210
8. Dember WN, Warm JS, Parasuraman R (2001) Olfactory stimulation and sustained attention. In: Compendium of olfactory research, pp 39–46
9. Arduino. https://arduino.cc. Last accessed 15 May 2023
10. Lukasiewicz MS, Spadoni E, Carulli M, Rossoni M, Dozio N, Ferrise F, Bordegoni M (June 2023) An open-source olfactory display to add the sense of smell to the metaverse. J Comp Inf Sci Eng, accepted (June 2023)
11. Unity 3D. https://unity.com. Last accessed 15 May 2023
12. Open XR Plugin. https://docs.unity3d.com/Packages/com.unity.xr.openxr@1.7/manual/index.html. Last accessed 15 May 2023
13. Meta Quest 2 headset. https://www.meta.com/it/en/quest/products/quest-2/. Last accessed 15 May 2023
14. Olfactory Display. https://github.com/virtual-prototyping-lab/olfactory-display-for-metaverse. Last accessed 15 May 2023
15. Lorenzo G, Oblinger D, Dziuban C (2007) How choice, co-creation, and culture are changing what it means to be net savvy. Educause Q 30:6–12
16. Golonka EM, Bowles AR, Frank VM, Richardson DL, Freynik S (2014) Technologies for foreign language learning: a review of technology types and their effectiveness. Comp Assist Lang Learn 27:1, 70–105
17. Bennett S, Maton K (2010) Beyond the 'digital natives' debate: towards a more nuanced understanding of students' technology experiences. J Comp Assist Learn 26:321–331
18. Prensky M (2001) Digital natives, digital immigrants. On the Horizon 9:1–6
19. Bialystok E, Miller B (1999) The problem of age in second-language acquisition: influences from language, structure, and task. Bilingualism: Lang Cogn 2:2, 127–145
20. Birdsong D (2005) Interpreting age effects in second language acquisition. In: Kroll J, de Groot AMB (eds) Handbook of bilingualism: psycholinguistic approaches. Oxford University Press, New York, pp 109–127
21. Brill J, Park Y (2008) Facilitating engaged learning in the interaction age taking a pedagogically-disciplined approach to innovation with emergent technologies. Int J Teach Learn High Educ 20
22. Kesima M, Ozarslan Y (2012) Augmented reality in education: current technologies and the potential for education. Procedia—Soc Behav Sci 47:297–302
23. Saidin NF, Noor DAH, Yahaya N (2015) A review of research on augmented reality in education: advantages and applications. Int Educ Stud 8:13
24. Nakamoto T (2013) Human olfactory displays and interfaces: odor sensing and presentation (Chaps. 1 and 3)
25. Sowndhararajan K, Songmun K (2016) Influence of fragrances on psychophysiological activity of human: with special reference to human electroencephalographic response. Sci Pharm 84:724–751
26. Vuforia. https://www.ptc.com/it/products/vuforia. Last accessed 15 May 2023
27. Watson MR, Akins KA, Spiker C, Crawford L, Enns JT (2014) Synesthesia and learning: a critical review and novel theory. Front Human Neurosci 8:98
28. Rizzo M, Eslinger PJ (1989) Colored hearing synesthesia: an investigation of neural factors. Neurology 39(6):781
29. Nerurkar NK, Chitnis TA, Pereira J (2022) Presence and pattern of chromesthesia in 200 individuals: an experiment performed on world voice day. Int J Phonosurg Laryngol 12(1):12–15

30. Kuo YT, Chuang MC (2013) A proposal of a color music notation system on a single melody for music beginners. Int J Music Educ 31(4):394–412
31. Wong M, Danesi M (2015) Color, shape, and sound: a proposed system of music notation. Semiotica 2015(204):419–428
32. Caivano JL (1994) Color and sound: physical and psychophysical relations. Color Res Appl 19(2):126–133
33. Logic Pro. https://www.apple.com/logic-pro/. Last accessed 15 May 2023

Chapter 8
Connecting Reality and Virtuality

Abstract This chapter presents three examples that demonstrate the effective integration of Reality and Virtuality, resulting in captivating applications that significantly enhance and improve the user experience through their seamless combination. The primary objective of the first case study is to explore and examine various methods of fostering connections among individuals through the utilization of Augmented Reality technology for collaborative art experiences. The second case study focuses on proposing a connection between humans and plants through Virtual Reality to enhance mental and physical well-being, as well as overall quality of life. The third case study focuses on leveraging Augmented Reality technology for maintenance operations.

8.1 Connecting People: Augmented Reality Application for Collaborative Art

Objective: Design a socially engaging and interactive experience where virtual data associated with a public artwork dynamically adjusts based on real-time information gathered from surrounding environment.

Description: In the last years, public art has been influenced by new technological means, allowing an enhancement in exhibition visitors' personal and social expression. New technologies have placed a shift in the role of the visitor, allowing an active involvement in the creation of the work of art not yet just limited to passive fruition. In particular, among the new technologies, Augmented Reality (AR) is often used with the aim of involving visitors in stories that would otherwise be invisible. Considering the adoption of AR technology in the public art field, the case study presents *MoodShaper*, an AR application with the purpose of creating virtual public artwork based on the collective contributions of people. During the visitor's engagement with the public artwork, they have the opportunity to actively participate by incorporating a virtual object that represents their current mood and emotional state. The objective of this experience is to generate a collective artistic representation of emotional states within the public sphere. These representations are visualized using AR technology and dynamically evolve in real-time based on the user's data.

M. Bordegoni et al., *Prototyping User eXperience in eXtended Reality*,
PoliMI SpringerBriefs, https://doi.org/10.1007/978-3-031-39683-0_8

Requirements: The application's main requirements concern:

- Leveraging Augmented Reality technology to exhibit virtual objects that dynamically evolve based on real-time data collected within the actual environment.
- Utilizing technology to enrich self-expression and foster a sense of social belonging within the realm of art.

Concept: The concept of the application is influenced by notable cases from recent years that demonstrate the emerging possibilities and impact of technology in the realm of public art and creativity. One such example is "Unnumbered Sparks," a physical sculpture transformed into an interactive artwork that can be controlled by the crowd [1]. Visitors have the ability to modify the artwork in real-time using their mobile devices. Another inspiring instance that highlights the integration of AR technology in the artistic context is "WEARINMOMA" [2]. This project showcases how AR inclusion in public physical spaces empowers visitors to engage with and reshape art through the utilization of technology.

Continuing with the subject of AR, in 2021, an Augmented Gallery experience enabled visitors to exhibit AR paintings sourced from prominent institutions in London. This unique experience took place outdoors, providing a free and accessible environment for all to enjoy [3].

Built upon these principles, *MoodShaper* introduces an AR social and interactive experience that allows individuals to actively participate in the creation of collective art sculptures throughout the city, by sharing their real-time moods and emotional states. Through the utilization of an AR smartphone application, users can visualize the public art sculpture in AR and engage with it by making personal contributions. The AR public sculpture is composed of distinct, uncomplicated objects that individuals can incorporate to shape the final collective artwork. Each user has the freedom to customize the shape and color of their virtual objects before adding them to the sculpture, reflecting their current mood during the experience. Furthermore, users are responsible for determining the position of their objects within the AR sculpture.

Design: The collaborative art sculpture is brought to life through the user's individual expression, and it would not exist without their willingness to share their emotional state with others. In this generative process, the user assumes a crucial role and is considered an active participant in shaping the meaning of the experience. Moreover, the incorporation of AR technology allows for the revelation of intangible and hidden elements, such as the users' emotional states, which would otherwise be impossible to visualize without the aid of technology.

To access and customize the AR content, users are required to utilize a mobile application that scans an image marker situated within the chosen public space designated for the art installation. The decision to employ a mobile application stems from the desire to provide people with a convenient means of experiencing public artwork, without the need for any additional technological equipment besides their personal smartphones.

The AR application encompasses two primary functionalities:

- Explore the public artwork: This feature enables users to visualize the public artworks crafted in AR, providing an immersive experience of the virtual creations.
- Contribute to the public artwork: The second function allows users to actively participate in the artwork by incorporating a personalized virtual object, thereby making their own unique contribution to the collective artwork.

Regarding the second functionality, the process of generating the virtual object to be incorporated into the artwork occurs automatically, aligning with the user's current mood. To achieve this, the user is prompted to respond to a series of questions pertaining to their emotional state during the experience. Each question is accompanied by a graphical slider interface, allowing the user to interactively select their preferred value along the spectrum. Every question in the questionnaire is associated with a specific parameter that influences the shape and color of a 3D virtual cube. The user's choices made through the sliders determine the values for these parameters. As a result, the final shape and color of the cube accurately reflect the user's individual mood, dynamically changing based on the selected values. The questions and the corresponding parameters that are changed in the virtual object are represented in Table 8.1.

Once all the questions have been answered, the user has the ability to directly place the personalized virtual object anywhere within the real environment, adding and aligning it with the public artwork. The public art installation undergoes real-time updates based on the newly inserted user data. This ensures that the artwork remains responsive and evolves in accordance with the collective moods of the community, aiming to depict the social sentiment and emotional state of the community at a given moment. Figure 8.1 illustrates the step-by-step process of generating a new virtual object for contribution to the public artwork.

Table 8.1 Questions to assess the user's mood/emotional state and the corresponding modification of the virtual object

Questions to assess the users' mood/emotional state	Corresponding change of the virtual object
Do you currently feel calm?	Intensity of the noise
Have you experienced frequent laughter or smiling today?	Scale of the shape
Have you experienced a significant amount of anger throughout the day?	Roughness level of the noise
How challenging has your day been up until now?	Number of vertices of every shape
How grateful are you feeling today?	Color hue of the shape
Rate the extent of happiness you have experienced today	Saturation level of the shape's color
Have you found yourself complaining frequently today?	Color brightness of the shape

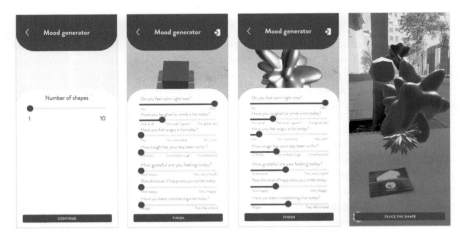

Fig. 8.1 Procedure for creating a new virtual object to make a contribution to the public artwork

Technology: The AR application has been specifically designed for mobile devices. Unity 3D was utilized as the development platform for creating the AR application [4], while the Vuforia SDK Plugin was integrated to incorporate AR functionalities [5]. To enable basic interactions such as object translation, the Lean Touch Asset was downloaded from the Unity Assets Store and integrated into the application [6]. The graphical user interface (GUI) of the application was initially designed using Figma [7] before seamlessly integrating the graphical elements within Unity 3D.

Architecture: Figure 8.2 displays the information architecture of the application, which consists of eight distinct sections.

Upon launching the application, the *Splash page* showcasing the application name will automatically appear for a duration of five seconds. Subsequently, the *Scan the AR marker* page will be presented to the user. Here, the user can click on a button to activate their device's camera and align it with the physical marker associated with the public art installation. After successfully completing this step, another page will be displayed, providing the user with the option to select between two functions: *explore the AR public artwork* or *contribute to the AR public artwork*.

Upon selecting the desired function, two distinct interaction flows are initiated. Opting for the first function activates the device's camera, enabling the user to see the AR public artwork superimposed on the real environment. This grants the user the ability to observe the artwork from various perspectives and grasp the collective mood expressed through the shapes and colors of the virtual objects. Conversely, selecting the second function initiates the flow for creating the AR virtual object, granting the user the opportunity to customize the virtual object based on their mood and add it to the public artwork within the environment.

Implementation: To establish the interactions and connections among the application screens, a low-fidelity prototype was developed after designing the user flow. This

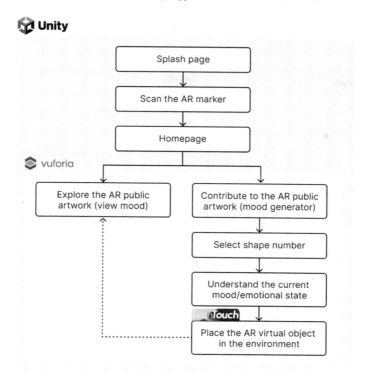

Fig. 8.2 Information architecture of the *MoodShaper* AR application

involved designing all the GUI elements using Figma and subsequently importing them into Unity3D. In the next phase, multiple scripts were generated to create the initial 3D object presented to the user and to control its customization, enabling modifications to the shape and color.

In order to generate the virtual object and provide the ability to subsequently modify its shape, the Procedural Mesh Generation Method was employed. This method involves generating a mesh consisting of interconnected vertices that form triangles. Figure 8.3 illustrates the step-by-step process employed to create each mesh.

The initial step involved identifying the three axes of the plane on which the mesh would be constructed, followed by considering the resolution (r), which determines the number of vertices present on each dimension of the mesh (in this example, r corresponds to 3).

Starting from the value of r, the number of squares was calculated, which is equal to $(r - 1)^2$. This, in turn, determined the total number of triangles, as each square is composed of two triangles. Since each triangle is comprised of three vertices, the total number of vertices in the mesh is equivalent to the number of triangles multiplied

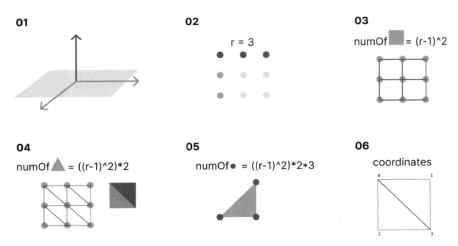

Fig. 8.3 Process for creating each mesh that comprises the 3D virtual object

by 3. To generate the individual triangles that constitute the mesh and connect them together, the coordinates of each vertex were calculated.

The Procedural Mesh Generation Method was utilized to create the six meshes composing the initial virtual shape resembling a cube. To facilitate future modifications and achieve complex shapes, the resolution (r) was set as a maximum value of 256, and all points on the mesh were normalized to face the same direction.

After creating the initial virtual object, additional scripts were implemented to alter its shape and color, with the corresponding values linked to the previously designed GUI sliders. Numerous tests were conducted at this stage to refine and attain the final outcome.

Subsequently, the Vuforia SDK Plugin was employed to implement the AR. Given the concept of creating multiple public artworks across the city, two markers representing different locations in the city of Milan were utilized to test the system's adaptability to various public spaces. The image markers utilized are depicted in Fig. 8.4.

Each image marker was utilized in two distinct Unity scenes, serving the purpose of showcasing both the complete AR public artwork and the individual AR object personalized by the user. Upon creating a new virtual object, it is immediately cloned into the scene associated with the overall public artwork and linked to the corresponding image marker.

For the prototype's implementation, the virtual objects created are stored directly within the application. However, in future developments, it is possible to establish a database on a cloud server to store and retrieve the virtual objects. This would allow for better scalability and management of the virtual objects in the application.

Furthermore, users are empowered to position the virtual object in alignment with the public artwork by simply dragging and dropping it via the touch screen of their device. To facilitate this interaction, the Lean Touch external Asset was

Fig. 8.4 Image markers created to showcase the public artwork within two distinct public spaces located in the city of Milan

incorporated, and the accompanying scripts were activated specifically during the interactive moments, enabling the seamless implementation of this intuitive user experience.

Upon completing the instantiation of the initial virtual object within the real environment, users are granted the opportunity to augment the public artwork further by adding additional virtual objects. To facilitate this option, a design decision was made to prompt users at the beginning of the experience to specify the desired number of objects they intend to create. This approach enables the resetting of script values associated with virtual object creation, allowing for iterative iterations to occur as many times as indicated by the user's input.

Credits: Students: Andrej Lazarovski, Polina Bobrova, Jose Alvaro, and Flores Gambarelli, Virtual and Physical Prototyping course, School of Design, Politecnico di Milano, Academic Year 20/21.

Video Youtube: https://youtu.be/ZapCL-_ku24

8.2 Bonding with Nature: Multisensory VR Application for Humans and Plants Well-Being

Objective: Create a multisensory experience exploiting eXtended Reality technology, with the aim of improving humans' mental and physical well-being and increasing the life quality.

Description: In today's fast-paced world, people's busy lifestyles often result in increased stress and anxiety. Many find it challenging to prioritize self-care and mental and physical well-being due to daily commitments. The pandemic has further exacerbated this stressful situation, particularly for vulnerable individuals who may experience social isolation, increased workload, and limited socioeconomic resources, leading to heightened stress levels and reduced life satisfaction [8]. To contrast this, people are increasingly focusing on self-care to counterbalance the negative effects of stress and anxiety and improve their psychophysical health. Self-care involves participating in activities that promote wellness and positive emotions for better physical and emotional health [9]. To achieve this, individuals have adopted various techniques, including connecting with nature and practicing relaxation using meditation and yoga. Studies have shown that exposure to natural environments has a positive impact on mental and physical health [10], increasing self-esteem and mood while reducing anger and other negative emotions and behaviors [11, 12]. The *Ajana* project emphasizes individual well-being by promoting a link between humans and plants to restore mental and physical health. This is done through a multisensory Virtual Reality application that monitors vital parameters in real-time using various sensors. The relationship between humans and plants is intended to reduce stress levels, lower cortisol levels, and create a deep connection with nature, resulting in an overall increase in well-being.

Requirements: The application's design must fulfill the following criteria:

- it should be portable;
- it should be effortless to configure and operate;
- real-time data collection is necessary;
- the virtual environment must adapt and modify based on the gathered information.

Concept: There has been a growing interest in mobile technologies to help the self-management of stress, anxiety, and mood. Some research illustrates that eXtended Reality technologies have the potential to provide interactive and body-based innovations for meditation practices [13]. Especially several solutions present the integration of Augmented Reality (AR) and Virtual Reality (VR) technologies with the aim of facilitating people's relaxation [14, 15]. Other solutions use mobile devices to create human-nature connections and promote physical well-being. As an example, Plant Wave is a device that catches the electrical pulses produced by plants to create sound with the aim of inducing a state of relaxation [16].

Various research has indicated that the closeness between individuals and nature can enhance the well-being of both. Bratman et al. [17] conducted a study where individuals' stress levels were observed as they traversed various routes, revealing that those who walked through leafy streets were less stressed than those who walked on barren streets. Another study found a stronger reduction in systolic blood pressure when participants could view an expanse of plants resembling a meadow, opposed to bare land without vegetation [18].

Ajana is a VR application that seeks to foster a deeper bond between humans and nature, as well as empowering individuals to monitor and leverage their stress levels in real-time. Furthermore, *Ajana* presents an opportunity to enrich self-awareness and acquire practical methods for attaining a state of calmness. By utilizing sensors installed on both the user and the plant, the application collects real-time data on the individual's stress levels and the plant's electric activity. It is designed for young adults and incorporates a blend of visual and auditory components to deliver a multi-sensory experience.

Design: The *Ajana* application is meant to be used in a tranquil setting surrounded by vegetation while sitting beside a plant. While engaging with the application, the user wears a Head Mounted Display (HMD), and a Photoplethysmography (PPG) sensor on their finger, which is used to measure the stress levels. The plant is fitted with Electrodermal Activity (EDA) sensors on its leaves, which are used to measure their electrical variations. The HMD displays a virtual environment that reflects a natural setting (Fig. 8.5). The PPG sensor tracks the user's stress level by monitoring oxygen levels, blood pressure, and heart rate. Stress triggers a mechanism that reduces blood flow to the body's peripheral pathways, leading to reduced oxygenation, which is detected by the PPG sensor for measuring the volumetric variation of blood circulation. Furthermore, utilizing the PPG sensor allows for the measurement of heart rate, which escalates as stress levels rise. An Electrodermal Activity sensor (EDA) measures electrical pulses inside the plant via electrodes on its leaves, enabling the assessment of stimuli the plant receives from its surroundings. By continuously monitoring the user's oxygen levels in real-time, it becomes possible to detect three different stages of stress. Consequently, the virtual environment adjusts to the user's present stress level, while the electrical signals produced by the plant result in distinctive audio and visual stimuli.

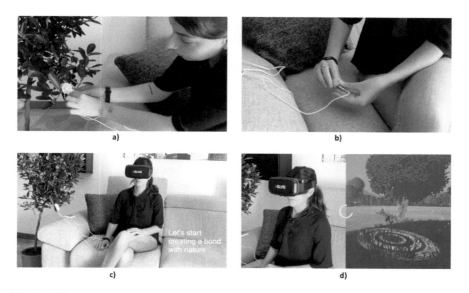

Fig. 8.5 The *Ajana* application can be utilized through: **a** attaching sensors onto the leaves of plants; **b** wearing PPG sensors on the fingers; **c** fostering a connection with nature through the application; **d** viewing the virtual world via HMD

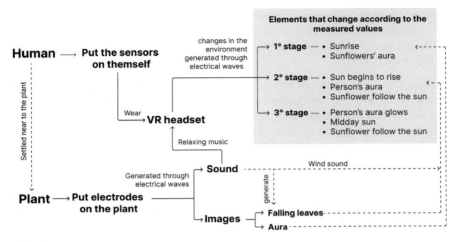

Fig. 8.6 *Ajana* system and virtual environment stages related to the acquired data

The interplay between user and plant influences the virtual environment, resulting in distinct stages for each level as shown in Fig. 8.6.

When experiencing a high level of stress, the virtual environment showcases a soothing sunrise with warm colors that trigger a sense of relaxation based on the circadian rhythm theory. Furthermore, the system generates calming music through real-time plant data, and a sunflower with an energy aura appears to enhance the atmosphere. If the stress level is moderate, the sunflower in the virtual setting follows the sun's movement, accompanied by an aura that indicates a revitalization of energy and decreased stress. The sound effects from the plant's waves combine with falling leaves from the sky to promote tranquility. When stress is at a low level, the virtual environment illuminates with bright colors as the sun sits high in the sky during midday. The user's aura glows to signify their strong energy.

Technology: A Bitalino board was used to collect bio data and signals from the plant [19]. A Bitalino board is a small, open-source hardware platform designed for creating and prototyping DIY projects related to biometrics, physiology, and other health-related applications. It consists of various sensors, such as electrocardiography (ECG), electromyography (EMG), and electrodermal activity (EDA) sensors, as well as a microcontroller, Bluetooth, and a rechargeable battery. Bitalino boards can be programmed using various software tools, including Python and Arduino, and they can be used to develop applications in fields such as healthcare, fitness, sports, and robotics. In the *Ajana* application, PPG sensors were used to acquire human bio signals, and electrodes and EDA sensors were used to measure electrical pulses inside the plant. The virtual environment was created using Unity 3D [20] and a connection was established with the Bitalino board.

Architecture: The system architecture is composed by the following main elements (Fig. 8.7): an HMD and the Bitalino board and sensors that are connected to the

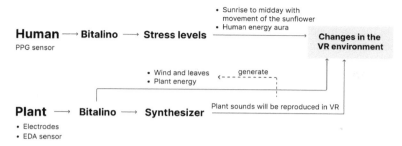

Fig. 8.7 *Ajana* application architecture

Unity 3D application. A GUI is included to initialize the application, connect the Bitalino and the sensors and start the data acquisition.

Implementation: Initially, Unity3D and Bitalino were linked through Bluetooth using the Bitalino API. A script was created to save the real-time readouts. The script also linked the readouts with the user's stress level and plant parameters. Three ranges were set, with varying values for humans and plants. The human stress levels were related to the heart rate and categorized into three ranges: the highest level was between 3000 and 651 Hz, the mid-level was between 650 and 450 Hz, and the lowest level was between 449 and 0 Hz. Based on the measured vital parameters of the plant, three different soundtracks and animations were utilized to enrich the immersive virtual environment. In relation to the plant parameters, for the high level of electrical pulses, the range was set between 0 and 50 Hz; for the mid-level of electrical pulses between 51 and 60 Hz; and for the low level of electrical pulses, between 61 and 90 Hz.

The soundtracks that corresponded to the plant parameters range were created by using the protocol specified in the Biodata Sonification project [21]. This project employs an Arduino board to fabricate soundtracks from the vital parameters of a plant. The project features a circuit that detects the electrical signals produced in the plant, which are then transformed into MIDI messages—a sequence of electrical pulses that are decoded by a synthesizer to produce sound. The Garage Band software was then utilized to generate different melodies from the MIDI messages [22]. Ultimately, three soundtracks were created by combining the different MIDI signals, and these were incorporated into the virtual experience linked to the user's stress levels.

Using Unity 3D, a virtual world was created featuring a lake encircled by mountains and trees situated on a small island. The waterfall effect in the world fluidly mimics the movement of water. Also included in the environment are natural components such as grass and flowers to further enhance its realism. The environment was initially designed utilizing pre-existing assets obtained from the Unity Assets Store [6]. Additional elements, such as the aura and waterfall effects, were generated using Unity 3D's Particle System.

Numerous animations and scripts were developed to depict and oversee alterations in the environment based on gathered data. One noteworthy script facilitates management of the sun's movement throughout the day by setting specific positions and hues at daybreak, morning, and noon, based on the human stress level. To assist users during the initialization phase and provide experience recommendations, a GUI was created using Figma [7] and integrated into Unity 3D.

Credits: Students: Nicole Beatrice Bonacina, Lorenzo Sindoni, Virtual and Physical Prototyping course, School of Design, Politecnico di Milano, Academic Year 20/21.

Video Youtube: https://youtu.be/bx8-y-2Fq4E

8.2.1 Utilizing Augmented Reality for Maintenance of 3D Printers

Objective: Employing Augmented Reality technology for the design and creation of an application enhancing maintenance operations for 3D Printers.

Description: The implementation of Augmented Reality in industrial training and maintenance tasks could make it possible for users to be trained and actively assisted during their performance without needing to refer to complex manuals or electronic technical support. As an example, 3D printer maintenance could represent a complex task given the number and complexity of required actions and the difficulties in understanding detailed printed manuals, especially for not expert users. The case study describes the implementation of an AR application for the maintenance of a Stratasys J700 Dental 3D printer [23] with the aim of helping users promptly understand the operations and supporting the industrial maintenance procedures. To implement and evaluate the AR application using actual machine components, a physical prototype replicating the 3D printer has been constructed.

Requirements: The main requirements for the design of the application are as follows:

- Enhancing comprehension of maintenance operations on an industrial machine through AR technology.
- Consulting the machine's maintenance manual for task sequence and requirements.
- Developing a user-friendly application accessible to non-experts.
- Offering real-time feedback on the accuracy of maintenance actions performed.

Concept: due to their complex composition, 3D printers pose a challenge as they consist of multiple components that demand skilled users and regular consultation of detailed maintenance protocols, component specifications, and safety instructions. These essential resources are primarily provided in complex printed manuals. Throughout maintenance procedures, this factor necessitates a continuous shift of user attention from the operational area to separate documentation. Furthermore, the reliance on conventional media for maintenance instructions often involves lengthy textual information that is challenging to present directly within the relevant area of interest using conventional techniques such as printed manuals or laptops [24].

The utilization of AR in maintenance applications has demonstrated positive outcomes in terms of task efficiency, operational management, and support for managerial decision-making [25]. AR technology enables the synthesis of complex sequences, presenting information through visual guidelines that integrate instructions and assistance directly within the task domain. It allows users to refer to the equipment they are inspecting, enhancing their ability to comprehend and perform maintenance tasks effectively.

The case study consists of an AR-based application to support users in some maintenance tasks on the *Stratasys J700 Dental* 3D Printer. The printing unit of the 3D printer consists of two key components: printing heads responsible for dispensing liquid resin, and UV lamps necessary for post-hardening the resin. Considering these functional elements, the AR application targets four specific maintenance procedures for the 3D printer:

- Calibration and replacement of UV lamps
- Replacement of printheads
- Cleaning process for printheads
- Resuming a paused print job.

The maintenance manual for this 3D printer, available for free on the manufacturer's website, serves as the primary source of information for the maintenance procedures. The manual is structured as an extensive collection of folders and subfolders, providing comprehensive details on the procedures. To present this information to users, the application employs a Graphical User Interface (GUI) and utilizes AR animations to highlight the relevant physical components that require attention during the procedures.

Design: To assess the functionality of the AR application for maintenance operations, a physical replica of the 3D printing unit has been constructed. This replica simplifies the actual machine, featuring only the necessary components for the designated tasks, including printheads (numbered 2) and UV lamps (numbered 1 and 3), as depicted in Fig. 8.8.

The actual printing unit operates across two axes on the printing plate, with the vertical axis responsible for vertical displacement. This coordinated movement enables the material to be deposited in a three-dimensional structure. To simplify the physical replica, the motion of the unit has been limited to a single axis. For tracking purposes in the AR application, an image marker has been employed. This image marker is affixed to the physical recreation of the printheads, ensuring accurate instantiation of the AR content.

The AR-based application, to be installed and used on a tablet, features a homepage where users can access maintenance processes by clicking on four interface

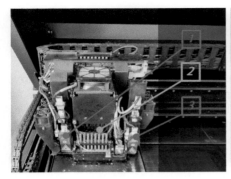

Fig. 8.8 Actual components of the 3D printer (on the left) and physical replica of the printing unit (on the right) consisting of printheads (2) and the UV lamps (1, 3)

buttons. Once a maintenance process is selected, the application presents the necessary devices and safety rules to be followed during the procedure. The device's camera is then activated, prompting the user to perform a series of step-by-step operations indicated by AR animations overlaying the components of the physical replica. To assist the user, a 2D avatar provides both textual and audio instructions for each operation, ensuring the correct sequence is followed. The user is always prompted to confirm the completion of an operation before the next one is presented. After completing the maintenance process, the user is directed back to the main menu, where they can choose another maintenance process if desired.

Technology: The tablet application has been developed utilizing Unity 3D [20], while the integration of AR technology has been achieved through the adoption of the Vuforia Engine SDK [5]. Moreover, to create the physical prototype, an Arduino board [26] connected to an LCD display has been utilized to emulate the electronics of the 3D printer.

Architecture: The system comprises the physical replica of the Stratasys J700 Dental machine's printing unit and the accompanying AR application. The application's information architecture consists of a Homepage menu that allows users to select their desired task, along with four distinct interaction flows, each presenting a series of sequential actions (refer to Fig. 8.9).

Upon launching the application, users are greeted with a Homepage featuring an interface menu showcasing the four proposed tasks (Fig. 8.10).

Upon selecting one of the interface buttons, the respective flow associated with the chosen task initiates. At the beginning of each task, users are provided with information regarding the necessary safety tools (if applicable) and any potential safety concerns. Subsequently, the actions to be performed are presented in a sequential manner, utilizing AR animations and accompanying textual instructions, as depicted in Fig. 8.11.

The AR contents are accurately superimposed on the components of the physical replica, facilitated by the utilization of an image marker affixed to the replica, enabling

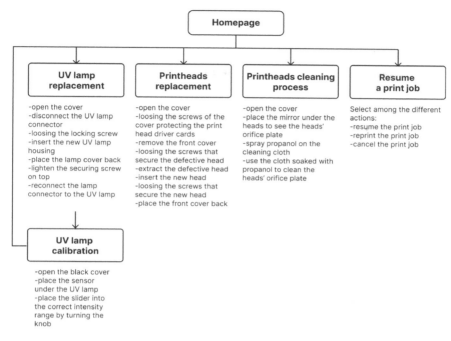

Fig. 8.9 Application information architecture

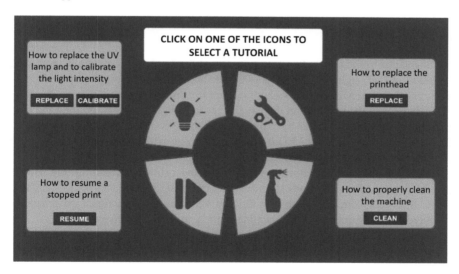

Fig. 8.10 App Homepage showing the four tasks to perform

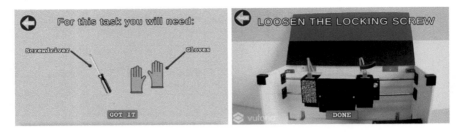

Fig. 8.11 Display depicting the recommended safety tools and an illustration of AR content exhibited on the physical replica of the actual machine

reliable AR tracking. Each task presented to the user consists of a varying number of steps. Once a step is completed, users can proceed to the next one by simply pressing the "DONE" button.

The replacement of UV lamps entails numerous complex steps, involving careful consideration of various elements. These lamps play a crucial role in curing the resin, but they have a limited lifespan despite their extended usage. Furthermore, after replacing a lamp, calibration is highly recommended to ensure its effective radiance falls within the specified range. The AR application assists in the lamp replacement process through informative animations, showcasing the required actions. Notably, 3D models of arrows and actual machine components, such as the cover and printheads, are primarily employed to indicate the necessary steps.

Once the UV lamp replacement is successfully accomplished, the user receives positive feedback and has the option to proceed with the UV lamp calibration task or return to the main Homepage menu. To facilitate the UV lamp calibration step, a simulated electronic system has been integrated into the physical replica. This system includes an LED light whose intensity can be adjusted by rotating a physical knob. The real-time intensity value is captured and transmitted to the tablet application. A GUI slider in the application displays the current light intensity, guiding the user to achieve the correct value by manipulating the physical knob, as illustrated in Fig. 8.12. Furthermore, the LED light changes color, with green indicating that the desired intensity has been achieved.

During the tasks of printhead replacement and printhead cleaning, the user is provided with AR instructions regarding the removal and replacement of machine parts. Similar to the UV lamp replacement task, these instructions are primarily displayed in AR directly on the machine replica, utilizing red arrows.

The task of resuming a paused print job is designed to assist the user in restarting a print job that was previously stopped. On the actual Stratasys J700 Dental machine, resuming printing is typically performed through the print manager using specialized software. To simulate the functionality of the real machine, a simplified version of the menu has been recreated using an LCD display and four physical buttons to

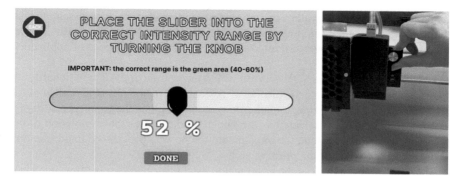

Fig. 8.12 The UV light calibration task is facilitated by a GUI slider and an LED light positioned on the physical replica

navigate within the functions. This recreated menu allows the user to choose from the following actions:

- Resume the print job;
- Reprint the print job;
- Cancel the print job.

Users can effortlessly navigate the software menu by utilizing the dedicated buttons located on the right side of the LCD display. The options are displayed simultaneously on both the LCD screen and the application interface. Furthermore, to provide enhanced guidance during task execution, additional text instructions are displayed on the screen (Fig. 8.13).

Implementation: The initial stage of the implementation involved the development of the AR application using Unity 3D. Within the same Unity project, distinct scenes were created to correspond to the various tasks to be performed. To populate the AR environment, several 3D models were crafted in a separate 3D modeling software. These models encompassed different arrow variations, the primary shell of the printing units, and simplified versions of the printheads. Additionally, interface

Fig. 8.13 LCD display utilized to replicate the functionality of the real display, synchronized with the corresponding application screen

elements such as a 2D avatar serving as a step-by-step guide and essential GUI components like panels and buttons were designed using Adobe Illustrator. Subsequently, all these elements were imported into Unity for the purpose of application development.

In addition, the Vuforia SDK was utilized to incorporate the AR functionality. To enable tracking and activate the display of AR content on the physical replica of the 3D printing machine, an image marker was employed. For the prototype, a highly recognizable image was selected as the image marker. After the completion of the AR application development, the implementation process progressed to the creation of the physical replica of the printing unit.

The primary framework of the printing unit was constructed using plywood, while the components of interest were 3D modeled and subsequently 3D printed for the prototype development (Fig. 8.14).

An Arduino board was integrated to facilitate control over various aspects, including the recreation of the UV light calibration system by incorporating the LED and knob, as well as simulating the printer software through the LCD display. To establish communication between Arduino and the Unity application, a serial connection was established. This allowed real-time data reading, enabling the updating of information displayed on both the physical components and the GUI application. For instance, during the UV light calibration procedure, a photoresistor was employed to read the light intensity, which was then transmitted to the application via Arduino. In the application, the analog signal from Arduino was converted to a percentage value, which was displayed on the GUI and refreshed as the user adjusted the physical knob. Additionally, the light intensity value was associated with the color of the physical LED light, providing dual feedback to the user. The Arduino board also controlled the LCD display and the connected physical buttons. Similar to the previous scenario,

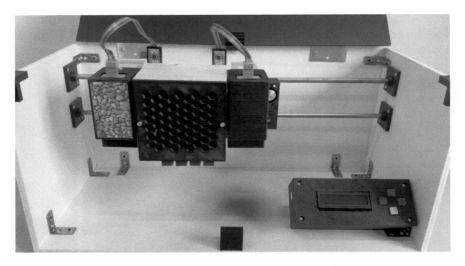

Fig. 8.14 Physical replica of the 3D printing unit

data from user inputs on the physical buttons were sent in real-time to both the LCD display and the GUI application.

Credits: Students: Dalila Di Palma and Luca Guida, Virtual and Physical Prototyping course, School of Design, Politecnico di Milano, Academic Year 21/22.

Video Youtube: https://youtu.be/VjECGJ-u9AA

References

1. Unnumbered Sparks. http://www.aaronkoblin.com/project/unnumbered-sparks/. Last accessed on 15 May 2023
2. WEARINMOMA. http://www.sndrv.nl/moma/. Last accessed on 15 May 2023
3. artoflondon. https://artoflondon.co.uk/events/augmented-reality-art-gallery. Last accessed on 15 May 2023
4. Unity-MARS. https://unity.com/products/unity-mars. Last accessed 15 May 2023
5. Vuforia. https://www.ptc.com/it/products/vuforia. Last accessed 15 May 2023
6. Unity Asset Store. https://assetstore.unity.com/. Last accessed 15 May 2023
7. Figma. https://www.figma.com. Last accessed 15 May 2023
8. Kuhn U, Klaas HS, Antal E, Dasoki N, Lebert F, Lipps O et al (2021) Who is most affected by the Corona crisis? An analysis of changes in stress and well-being in Switzerland. Eur Soc 23(sup1):S942–S956
9. Rupert PA, Dorociak KE (2019) Self-care, stress, and well-being among practicing psychologists. Prof Psychol Res Pract 50(5):343
10. Wolsko C, Lindberg K, Reese R (2019) Nature-based physical recreation leads to psychological well-being: evidence from five studies. Ecopsychology 11(4):222–235
11. Maller CJ (2009) Promoting children's mental, emotional and social health through contact with nature: a model. Health Educ 109:522–543
12. Kaplan R (2001) The nature of the view from home. Environ Behav 33:507–542
13. Döllinger N, Wienrich C, Latoschik ME (2021) Challenges and opportunities of immersive technologies for mindfulness meditation: a systematic review. Front Virtual Real 2:644683
14. Viczko J, Tarrant J, Jackson R (2021) Effects on mood and EEG states after meditation in augmented reality with and without adjunctive neurofeedback. Front Virtual Real 2:618381
15. Pallavicini F, Bouchard S (2019) Assessing the therapeutic uses and effectiveness of virtual reality, augmented reality and video games for emotion regulation and stress management. Front Psychol 10:2763
16. Plant Wave. https://plantwave.com/. Last accessed 15 May 2023
17. Bratman GN, Anderson CB, Berman MG, Cochran B, De Vries S et al (2019) Nature and mental health: an ecosystem service perspective. Sci Adv 5(7)
18. Lindemann-Matthies P, Matthies D (2018) The influence of plant species richness on stress recovery of humans. Web Ecol 18(2):121–128
19. Bitalino. https://www.pluxbiosignals.com/collections/bitalino. Last accessed 15 May 2023
20. Unity3D. https://unity.com. Last accessed 15 May 2023
21. Biodata Sonification project. https://www.instructables.com/Biodata-Sonification/. Last accessed 15 May 2023
22. Garage Band. https://www.apple.com/it/mac/garageband/. Last accessed on 15 May 2023
23. Stratasys Dental J700 3D. https://www.stratasys.com/en/3d-printers/printer-catalog/polyjet/j700-dental-printer. Last accessed 15 May 2023
24. Henderson SJ, Feiner SK (2007) Augmented reality for maintenance and repair (ARMAR), Distribution, pp 62

25. Palmarini R, Erkoyuncu JA, Roy R, Torabmostaedi H (2018) A systematic review of augmented reality applications in maintenance. Robot Comp Integr Manuf 49:215–228
26. Arduino Board. https://www.arduino.cc. Last accessed 15 May 2023

Chapter 9
Conclusions

Abstract This chapter provides final remarks on the book's content and explores the promising future of prototyping in product design, particularly with the advent of emerging technologies such as the metaverse and Artificial Intelligence, which offer significant possibilities and advancements for the prototyping process.

Product design is a multidimensional field that combines engineering, design, psychology, and other disciplines to create new and innovative products. A product is a combination of tangible and intangible elements that are sold for a monetary exchange but also provide value to consumers. Understanding the concept of a product is essential to fully grasp the role of product design in modern industry.

The preferences of product customers have evolved, with a growing demand for personalized products. Companies have adapted to this trend by designing and producing small quantities of customized products tailored to individual customers' needs. However, manufacturing customized products presents challenges such as increased costs, longer production times, scalability issues, and competition from mass producers. Despite these challenges, many companies continue to focus on producing customized products to deliver a unique and high-quality customer experience.

Functions, style, and usability are the three primary attributes of products. Functions refer to the technical operations performed by the product, while style pertains to the visual appearance or outer appearance of the product. Usability encompasses aspects such as ease of use, interactivity, learnability, and content relevance. Today, people not only value a product based on its function but also consider style and usability. The ability to customize both the appearance and functionality of a product is highly valued by users.

The product development process is crucial in bringing new products to market efficiently and meeting the needs and preferences of users. The process involves turning a market opportunity into a commercially available product through various activities, including concept development, product architecture definition, detailed design, and testing. The roles of engineers and industrial designers are instrumental in product development, with engineers handling technical aspects and industrial designers focusing on style and usability.

M. Bordegoni et al., *Prototyping User eXperience in eXtended Reality*,
PoliMI SpringerBriefs, https://doi.org/10.1007/978-3-031-39683-0_9

Product development faces several challenges, including the increasing complexity of products, differentiation from competitors, limited resources and time, the lack of tolerance for design flaws, and sustainability concerns. Companies must effectively manage these challenges by implementing appropriate methods and tools, focusing on unique elements that make their products worth buying, meeting customer expectations for attractive, user-friendly, and smart products, and designing for sustainable behavior.

The concept development stage is vital in the product development process, where industrial designers and common design methods are involved. Concept design involves creating detailed explanations of a product's form, function, and features based on market research and analysis of rival products. The book specifically emphasizes the significance of prototyping in the field of product design.

Prototyping plays a crucial role in product design, serving as a valuable tool for designers to explore, evaluate, and refine their ideas. It involves creating a physical or virtual representation of the product concept before moving into the production phase. Prototyping allows designers to test and validate their ideas, gather feedback from stakeholders, and make informed decisions throughout the product development process. The book thoroughly explores various key factors that underscore the significance of prototyping in the realm of product design, including idea exploration and visualization, iterative design and refinement, communication and collaboration, technical feasibility, and validation.

eXtended Reality (XR) technologies, such as Virtual Reality (VR) and Augmented Reality (AR), have revolutionized the field of prototyping in product design. By leveraging XR technologies, designers can create immersive and interactive virtual environments that simulate the look, feel, and functionality of a product before it is physically built. One of the key advantages of XR technologies in prototyping is the ability to visualize and experience products in a realistic and dynamic manner. Designers can use VR to create three-dimensional virtual models of products and simulate their usage scenarios, allowing for better evaluation of design choices and identifying potential issues early in the development process. AR enables designers to overlay virtual elements onto the real world, facilitating contextual evaluation and user interaction with virtual prototypes.

XR technologies enable rapid iteration and exploration of design alternatives. Changes to virtual prototypes can be made quickly and easily, allowing designers to experiment with various ideas, test different configurations, and gather valuable feedback from users early on. This iterative approach accelerates the design iteration cycle and enhances the overall design quality.

The book presents nine case studies developed by students who participated in the Virtual and Physical Prototyping course at the School of Design, Politecnico di Milano. These case studies highlight the potential and advantages of utilizing eXtended reality (XR) technologies for prototyping both physical and digital products in specific contexts. The examples demonstrate the diverse applications of XR technologies, including Augmented Reality and Virtual Reality, in promoting sustainability, creating multisensory experiences, and effectively integrating the real and virtual worlds. Each case study focuses on specific objectives and benefits associated with the use of these technologies in various fields. Furthermore, the book describes how the prototypes were implemented based on the guidelines outlined in Chap. 5.

The future of prototyping in product design is likely to be influenced by emerging technologies such as the Metaverse and Artificial Intelligence (AI). These advancements offer new possibilities and capabilities that can greatly enhance the prototyping process.

One potential direction is the integration of virtual prototyping within the Metaverse. The Metaverse is an immersive, interconnected virtual space where users can interact with digital representations of objects and environments in a collaborative way. By leveraging the Metaverse, product designers can develop virtual prototypes that faithfully replicate the appearance, tactile experience, and functionality of physical products, allowing them to easily share these prototypes with stakeholders such as manufacturers, customers, and users. This virtual prototyping method empowers designers to collect feedback, perform user testing, and iteratively enhance their designs within a virtual environment, thereby mitigating the need for substantial investments in physical production until the design has been thoroughly refined.

AI also has the potential to revolutionize prototyping in product design. Machine learning algorithms can analyze vast amounts of data to generate design solutions and recommendations, optimize product performance, and predict user preferences. AI-powered generative design tools can be used to quickly explore a multitude of design possibilities and propose innovative solutions. Additionally, AI can assist in automating certain aspects of the prototyping process, such as generating 3D models, simulating product behavior, or conducting virtual simulations.